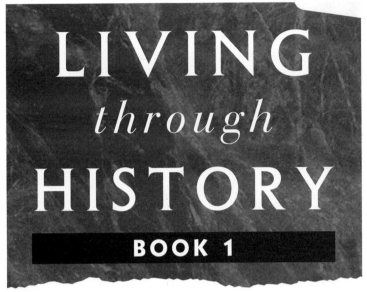

LIVING *through* HISTORY

BOOK 1

Foundation Edition

Roman Empire

Medieval Realms

Fiona Reynoldson
and
David Taylor

Heinemann

CONTENTS

The Roman Empire

Medieval Realms

The Romans lived hundreds of years ago. It is hard to find out about people who lived such a long time ago. There are two ways of finding out about the Romans.

1 Finding out from archaeology

Many things from Roman times have been covered by soil. **Archaeologists** dig up the ground to look for old things.

Archaelologists look for a good place to dig.

Lots of broken Roman pottery in this field.

What a find!

They could find the ruins of a Roman villa and lots of coins, jewellery etc.

Source A

Many Roman buildings were huge and have not fallen down. This shows how good the Romans were at building. The Romans built this stadium called the Colosseum. A lot of it is still standing.

Roman writing on stone found on Hadrian's Wall. It says that the Roman army built that part of the Wall.

Source B

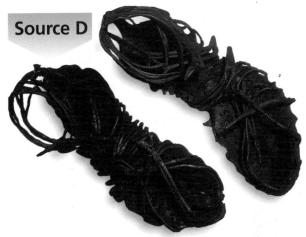

Archaeologists often find things which the Romans used every day. These are Roman sandals.

2 Finding out from Roman writing

a Writing on stone: We have found Roman carving and writing on stones. One soldier even carved rude names about the emperor on a wall. It was a good job that he was not found out!

b Books: We still have some books which were written by the Romans. They tell us a lot about how the Romans lived. The Romans wrote in Latin. So we have to translate what they wrote.

Source C

This Roman is writing about the Emperor Nero. Nero was dead when it was written, otherwise it would not have been so nasty.

At night he walks the streets looking for trouble. He used to stab men on their way home from dinner.

Nero also went shoplifting. Afterwards he set up a market stall to sell the goods he had stolen!

Questions

1 Read **Finding out from archaeology**. What do archaeologists do?

2 Read **Finding out from Roman writing**.

   a Which two kinds of writing have the Romans left us?
   b What language did the Romans use?

3 Look at Source A.

   a What was the Colosseum?
   b Why is a lot of it still standing?

4 Read Source C. Why did the writer of this source dare to be nasty about Nero?

Good fun!

Archaeologists do not just dig up things from the ground.

They also try to guess what these things were, and what they tell us about people in the past.

This is the fun part of their job.

Sometimes archaeologists find some very interesting things! (Look at Source A.)

Source A

Archaeologists often find some unusual things. This is a piece of human faeces, which is over a thousand years old! Archaeologists dug it up in York.

From looking at it, scientists can tell that the person had eaten a kind of bran and also had worms!

Lindow man

In 1984 workmen found a body in a peat bog at Lindow Moss, near Manchester.

The body was in very good condition. How long had it been in the bog?

Scientists carried out tests on the body. They said that the body had been in the bog since 500 BC!

The acid in the peat had kept the body in good condition. The scientists called the body Lindow man. (The workmen who found the body had called it Pete Marsh!)

Questions and more questions

Who was this man? What had happened to him? Why did he die? How did he die?

Scientists carried out some more tests to see if they could answer these questions.

What the tests showed

1 Lindow man had smooth finger nails. He might have made cloth. This would have smoothed his nails.

2 Fox hairs were found on his body. Perhaps he was wearing a fox fur to keep warm.

3 Bran and burnt wheat grains were found in Lindow man's stomach. He must have eaten a kind of bread just before he died.

4 Worms were also found in his stomach!

Question

Read Sources C and E on page 7. Why might Lindow man have been killed?

A nasty end!

The scientists found a rope around Lindow man's neck. He had probably been strangled. The body had some cuts on it as well.

It looks like Lindow man met a horrible death.

The body of Lindow man.

Source C

From a magazine article, 6 April 1997.

Lindow man had mistletoe juice in his stomach. We know that mistletoe was used when offerings were made to please a god. Lindow man could have been killed as a sacrifice to a god.

Source D

What a modern scientist says about the death of Lindow man.

He was knocked out so he could not fight back.

There is a wound in his head. It looks as if he was hit with an axe.

The rope cut into his neck. His neck was broken.

There is also a cut about two inches long over the jugular vein in the neck.

Source E

A historian's view about why Lindow man died.

He was completely naked. I think he was part of a sacrifice to a god. The area around Manchester is cold. He would not have been walking about naked out of choice!

1.3 CAN YOU ALWAYS TRUST HISTORICAL SOURCES?

Sources

Sources are things which tells us about the past. They give us clues or evidence. There are many different types of sources.

Problems with written sources

You cannot always trust what written sources say. They might not be telling the truth. Why is this?

1 The writer may not have known the exact truth.

2 The writer might be **biased** and only giving one side of the story.

Read the two newspaper reports on page 9. They are both reporting the same football match, but they each describe the match from their side only.

SUPER NEWCHESTER BEAT MANHAMPTON
Newchester 3 Manhampton 2

Newchester played brilliant football on Saturday.

They never stopped attacking the Manhampton goal and could have been several goals in the lead by half time.

In the second half Newchester were given two penalties. Dave Smith scored easily from both. The goalkeeper had no chance.

The Newchester forwards were much too fast for Manhampton. In the final minute, Jones headed the ball into his own goal to give Newchester a great win by 3–2.

Questions

1 Read **Newspaper A** and **Newspaper B**.

   a Which newspaper was printed in Newchester?

   b Which newspaper was printed in Manhampton?

   c How did you tell?

2 Why should we be careful when using written historical sources?

Be careful

A lot of the written sources in this book are by Romans.

Some of them might be telling the truth. But if they keep saying the Romans are great, they might be giving only one side of the story.

So take care!

Newspaper B

BRAVE MANHAMPTON ARE JUST BEATEN
Newchester 3 Manhampton 2

Manhampton were very unlucky to lose this match.

They were much the better team. Two great goals by Brown and Green put them 2–0 up at half time.

In the second half they scored two more goals. But the referee would not let them count. No one could see what was wrong with them.

The crowd could not believe it when the referee gave Newchester two penalty kicks. The Manhampton goalkeeper nearly saved them both.

In the final minute Newchester scored a shock winner. One of their players hit a hopeful shot. It was going well wide. But it hit the referee, bounced up into the face of Jones and went into his own goal.

It is the year AD 3000. Some students have been given a project to do called: 'Life in the 1990s'.

But they have a problem. There was an earthquake and nearly all the sources were lost. Only two sources were saved.

Source A

A photograph from the 1990s.

A photograph from the 1990s.

Questions

You are a student in AD 3000. You are trying to find out about 'Life in the 1990s'.

1 Look at Source A.
What sort of clothes did people wear in the 1990s?

2 Look at Source B.
What does it tell you about life in the 1990s?

3 What do Sources A and B not tell you about the 1990s?

Learning about history
Remember!

1 There are different kinds of **sources**. They give us clues (or evidence) about the past.

2 Written sources can be one-sided or biased.

3 Sometimes there are not enough sources to tell us the whole story.

What modern historians think

Historians think that Rome started near the river Tiber in Italy. There were seven villages, built on seven hills. Farmers lived in the villages. The villages grew together to become the city of Rome. This happened about 700 years before Jesus Christ was born.

Archaeologists have found pottery and round holes where the posts of the farmers' wooden huts used to be.

What the Romans said

The Romans told the story of Romulus and Remus to say how Rome started. You can read it on page 13. The story was passed down through the years.

Some of the story may be true, but other bits were made up to make it more exciting.

All Roman schoolchildren were told the story. The children loved to hear it. It made them think that Rome was a wonderful city. It made them proud to be Romans.

Rome was built on the river Tiber in Italy.

Source A

A statue of the she-wolf. She is feeding Romulus and Remus.

Questions

All the answers are on page 12.

1 In which country is Rome?

2 On which river was Rome built?

3 How do historians say Rome started?

4 What story did the Romans tell to say how Rome started?

5 Why were Roman schoolchildren told this story?

THE STORY OF ROMULUS AND REMUS

This is the story that was told to Roman children.

There was once a city called Alba Longa. It was on the banks of the river Tiber. It was ruled by King Numitor. He was driven from power by his wicked brother, Amulius.

Numitor's daughter was Rhea Silvia. She married Mars, the god of war. Rhea gave birth to twin boys. She called them Romulus and Remus.

Amulius was angry about this. He ordered the boys to be drowned. But the servant who was told to do this took pity on them. He left them floating in a cradle on the river.

The boys were found by a she-wolf. She let them feed on her milk. Then a shepherd found the boys. He took them home and brought them up.

When the boys grew up, they heard what Amulius had done to them. They were angry. They attacked Alba Longa. Amulius was killed.

Romulus and Remus said they would build a new city. They argued about where it should be built.

They agreed that whoever saw a vulture first in the sky could choose the place for the city. Remus said he saw a vulture first. But Romulus said he was the winner because he had seen twelve.

Romulus started to build the city on the Palatine hill. It had a wall around it. Remus was angry. He jumped over the wall to show that he did not think much of his brother's city. Romulus was so cross that he killed Remus.

The new city was finished in 753 BC. It was called Rome after Romulus.

Romulus was the first king of Rome. He died when he disappeared during a big storm. This happened in front of all the people of Rome.

Afterwards, Romulus became a god.

Rome ruled by kings

At first Rome was ruled by kings. The last king was called **Tarquinius Superbus** (Tarquin the Proud). The people did not like him. They drove him out of Rome in 509 BC.

Rome becomes a republic

The people said they did not want to be ruled by kings any more. Rome now became a **republic**. A republic is a place which does not have a king ruling.

Rome becomes powerful

Rome grew into the most powerful city in the world.

The Romans built a huge **empire**. An empire is when one country takes over and rules a lot of other countries.

The Roman Empire grew up slowly in four stages.

Stage 1: Rome takes over Italy

Rome started to take over other cities in Italy. By 265 BC Rome ruled most of Italy.

Roman land

ITALY
CORSICA
• Rome
SARDINIA
Mediterranean Sea
SICILY
Carthage •

0   300 miles
0   400 km

N
S

Rome ruled most of Italy by 265 BC.

HORATIUS THE HERO

The Romans loved to tell stories about brave people. One story was about a Roman soldier called Horatius Cocles (Horatio the One-Eyed).

Rome was being attacked by the Etruscans. They had to capture only one bridge to get into Rome. Horatius stopped the Etruscans from getting on to the bridge. He fought them off on his own. When he grew tired he jumped off the bridge and swam to the Roman side.

The Etruscans cheered but when they charged on to the bridge, it collapsed. They all fell into the river. The Romans had been chopping the bridge down while Horatius was fighting!

Horatius was a hero and was given a lot of land.

Stage 2: Rome beats Carthage

Carthage was a powerful city in north Africa. It ruled large parts of Africa and Spain. Carthage sold goods to the people who lived there.

Rome also started to sell goods to other countries. The Romans started to grow rich. Carthage did not like this. So the two cities went to war.

There were three wars between Rome and Carthage.

- **War 1 (264–241 BC).** The Romans won and took land from Carthage.
- **War 2 (218–201 BC).** Hannibal of Carthage took an army into Italy. The Romans beat him.
- **War 3 (149–146 BC).** The Romans burned the city of Carthage down. The Romans now ruled a big part of north Africa.

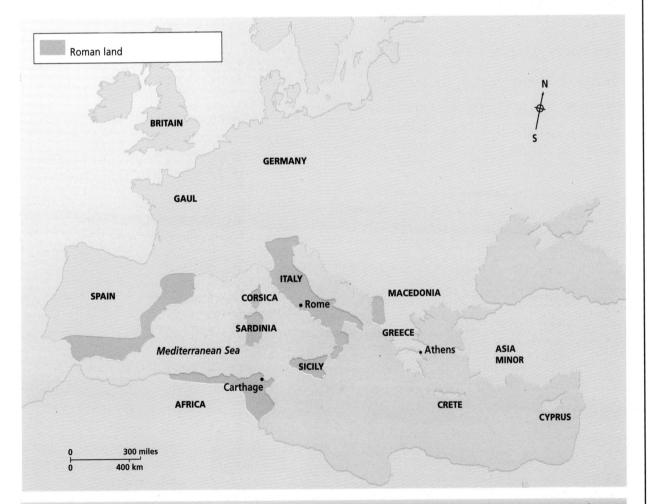

The start of the Roman Empire. This shows the land ruled by Rome after the second war against Carthage.

Stage 3: The Roman Empire grows

The Romans went on to capture more countries.

By **121 BC** the Romans had taken over Greece and Asia Minor (modern-day Turkey).

Stage 4: The Empire is completed

By **AD 120** the Romans had won more land in Asia, Africa and Britain. The Empire was now at its biggest.

Each country in the Empire was ruled by a Roman governor.

Each country was made to pay **taxes** to Rome.

Rome became very rich.

Source A

Written by a Roman historian.

The gods want Rome to be the most powerful city in the world.

No one will be able to beat the armies of Rome.

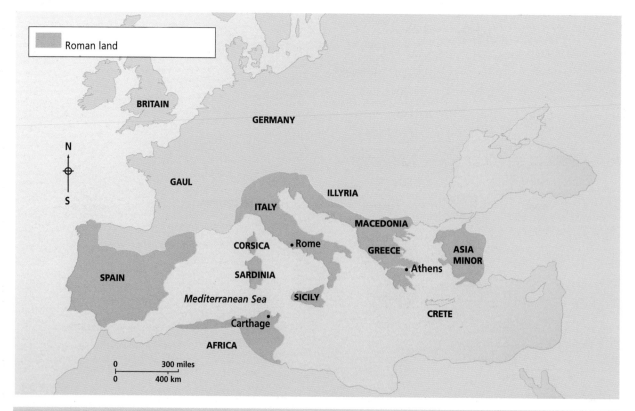

This was the size of the Roman Empire in 121 BC.

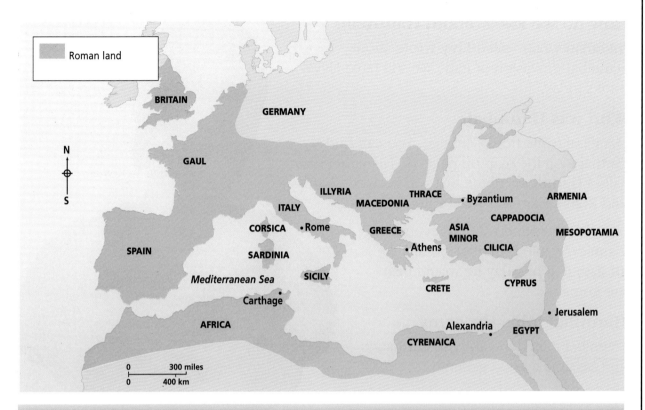

The Roman Empire at its biggest in AD 120.

No more land to be taken

In AD 120 Emperor Hadrian said the Empire was big enough. If it got any bigger, it would be too hard to run. Hadrian said that no more land was to be taken.

He built Hadrian's Wall across the north of Britain. The wall was the northern border of the Roman Empire.

The Empire is divided

As time went on, the Romans found it harder to defend the Empire from attack.

In AD 285 the Empire was divided into two parts. This made it easier to run and defend.

Questions

Read **Rome becomes powerful** on page 14.

1 Write out these sentences, filling in the gaps. Use the words from the box.

Rome grew into a powerful _____. It took over many _____ and made them part of the Roman _____.

countries	Empire	city

2 Look at page 15.
Which city did Rome beat?

3 Read **No more land to be taken** on page 17.

  a Who said no more land was to be taken?
  b Why did he say this?
  c What did he build across northern Britain?

How do we know about Hannibal?

A Roman writer called **Livy** wrote about Hannibal's invasion of Italy. We still have Livy's books today.

Who was Hannibal?

Hannibal came from Carthage. You can find Carthage on the map on page 19. His father was called **Hamilcar**. In the first war between Carthage and Rome, Hamilcar was beaten in battle.

He was angry and wanted revenge. Hamilcar made Hannibal swear an oath that one day he would beat the Romans.

Hannibal joins the army

Hannibal joined the army in Carthage and became a good general.

He was strong and brave.

Hannibal became the leader of the army.

Hannibal decides to invade Italy

In 218 BC a second war started between Carthage and Rome.

Hannibal decided to invade Italy. But he could not go across the sea because the Romans had a better navy. The Romans would be able to sink Hannibal's ships. Hannibal would have to go the long way round.

The journey to Italy

Hannibal said he would march through Spain and France. Then he would cross some large mountains called the Alps and march into Italy.

This was a journey of 1,500 miles. He set off with 100,000 men and 37 war elephants.

Source A

A statue of Hannibal.

It was found in a town in Italy.

LIVY (59 BC–AD 17)

Livy was a rich Roman. He wrote a book about the history of Rome. It was used a lot in Roman schools.

Some people do not trust what he wrote. This is because he told only the Roman side of the story.

Danger at every turn

On the journey, Hannibal had to fight off attacks from fierce tribes.

When they came to a big river, the elephants were floated across on huge rafts.

The Alps are reached

After crossing the river Rhône in France, they came to the Alps. Hannibal's men were frightened.

But Hannibal told them not to be cowards.

Huge rafts were used to get the elephants across rivers.

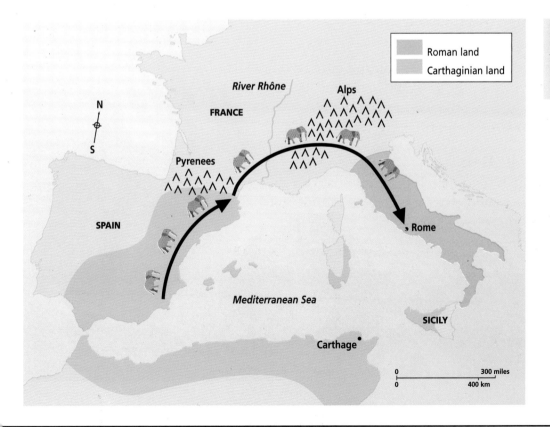

Hannibal's journey to Italy.

- Roman land
- Carthaginian land

River Rhône

Alps

FRANCE

N

S

Pyrenees

SPAIN

Mediterranean Sea

Rome

SICILY

Carthage

0 — 300 miles
0 — 400 km

Crossing the Alps

Hannibal's army struggled to the top of the mountains. It was hard going. Hannibal told his men it would be easier on the way down.

But it turned out to be even harder! The path down was very steep. Many men and animals slipped and died.

Then a huge boulder blocked their way. The boulder was bigger than a house. There seemed to be no way round it.

It looked as if their journey was at an end. But Hannibal had other ideas. His men started to break up the boulder (see box).

After the boulder had been broken up, the army was able to reach Italy.

It had taken them fifteen days to cross the Alps. Many men died on the way.

How the boulder was broken up

1 Vinegar was poured on to the boulder.

2 The acid in the vinegar helped to break up the boulder.

3 The men smashed the boulder with hammers.

4 After four days the boulder was smashed to pieces and the army was able to move on.

A modern painting of Hannibal's elephants crossing the Alps.

Source B

Panic in Rome

The people of Rome heard that Hannibal was on his way. They were very scared. But Hannibal did not have enough men or weapons to capture the city.

The Battle of Cannae

The Romans decided to fight Hannibal. But they were badly beaten in the Battle of Cannae.

Shocking scenes

There were terrible scenes after the battle. Thousands of Roman soldiers lay dying. They called out for people to cut their throats because they wanted to be put out of their misery.

At last Hannibal is beaten

By now Hannibal was running very short of supplies. So he had to go back to Carthage.

In 202 BC the Romans attacked Carthage. Hannibal was beaten in the fighting. Hannibal killed himself by taking poison.

The Romans celebrate

The Romans had been given a big scare by Hannibal. They were thankful he had not captured Rome.

For years afterwards, schoolchildren were told the story of Hannibal.

His name was used to frighten naughty children. Teachers would shout:

Hannibal is at the gates.

This soon made the children behave!

Questions

1 Read **The journey to Italy** on page 18.

   a Which mountains did Hannibal cross to get to Italy?

   b How many miles was his journey?

2 Look at page 19. How did they get the elephants across rivers?

3 Read **At last Hannibal is beaten**.

   a Why did Hannibal go back to Carthage?

   b How did he kill himself?

4 Read the box about **Livy** on page 18. Livy wrote about Hannibal's journey. Would you trust what he wrote?

Control of the Empire

People were frightened to fight the Romans. This was because the Romans had a very strong army. It hardly ever lost a battle. So the Romans kept control of the Empire.

Legions and centuries

- The biggest group in the Roman army was the **legion**.

- A legion had about 5,000 soldiers. They were called **legionaries**.

- A legion was commanded by a **legate**.

- A legion was divided into ten **cohorts**.

- A cohort was divided up into six **centuries**. Each century was under the command of a **centurion**.

Standards

Each century had its own badge or **standard**.

It was carried by the best soldier in the century.

It was a great honour to carry the standard.

Each legion also had a imperial standard, which was an eagle.

It was carried into battle by a standard-bearer. If the standard was captured in battle, it was a huge disgrace.

Source A

Written by a Roman in the 1st century AD.

A centurion called Luculius was killed by his own men. They hated him because he was so cruel.

The men called him 'give me another', because this is what he said each time he broke a stick hitting a soldier.

How to make a Roman legion

Step 1   Take eight men and form them into a group called a tent.

Step 2   Join ten tents together into a century of 80 men under the command of a centurion.

Step 3   Put six centuries together to make a cohort of 480 men.

CENTURY	CENTURY	CENTURY
1	2	3
CENTURY	CENTURY	CENTURY
4	5	6

Step 4   Put ten cohorts together to make 4,800 men. Add about 500 clerks and skilled tradesmen and you have a legion.

How the Roman army was organised.

Javelin: Made out of wood with a metal tip. About two metres long.

A modern painting of a Roman legionary in full uniform, with his equipment.

Helmet: Made of iron to protect the head.

Metal jacket: Very heavy. Made of strips of metal held together by leather straps.

Sword: About 50 cm long. It had a wooden handle and was worn in a **scabbard**.

Belt: This held the sword and dagger.

Tunic: Made of rough wool.

Shield: Made of wood with metal in the middle. About 1.6 metres tall.

Sandals: Made of leather. They had hob nails in the sole for marching.

Equipment: Each soldier had to carry his weapons, tools and blankets.

Joining the Roman army

There were three sorts of soldiers in the Roman army:

Centurions ·

Legionaries and

Auxiliaries

Becoming a legionary

To become a legionary a person had to be:

A Roman citizen

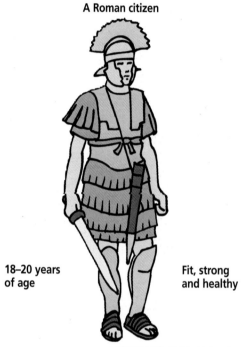

18–20 years of age

Fit, strong and healthy

Each legionary had to swear an oath of loyalty. They joined up for 25 years.

Training legionaries

The centurions trained the legionaries and were often very cruel to them. The training was very hard, so the legionaries had to be very fit and strong.

Three times a month the legionaries were sent on long marches. They were made to carry heavy packs. It was very tiring.

Legionaries were taught to:

- march in straight lines
- use a sword and shield
- throw the javelin.

Auxiliaries

Some soldiers in the army were called **auxiliaries**. They were soldiers who came from countries the Romans had conquered.

Special skills

The auxiliaries had special skills. They were very good at:

- fighting on horseback
- using a bow and arrow
- using a sling to shoot stones
- fighting with a sword.

Duties

Auxiliaries were used for patrolling and making quick raids on the enemy.

They were not as well trained as the legionaries. So they did not fight in big battles.

Length of service

Auxiliaries served for 25 years. When they left the army, they could become Roman citizens.

Source D

The tombstone of Marcus Favonius Facilis.

MARCUS FAVONIUS FACILIS

- Facilis was a centurion in the Twentieth Legion.

- His tombstone was found near Colchester.

- It had been broken into pieces, but it has been mended.

- It gives us a good idea of the uniform worn by a centurion.

- He has the centurion's stick in his right hand. The stick was used for beating soldiers.

Questions

1 Look at the picture on page 23.

   a Write down three weapons carried by a Roman legionary.
   b Write down three things which he had for protection.
   c Why did his sandals have hobnails in them?

2 Read **Training legionaries**.

   a Who trained the legionaries?
   b What was the training like?

3 Read Source A on page 22.
   Why was Luculius killed by the soldiers?

4 Read **Standards** on page 22.
   What was a standard?

Good discipline

The Romans were very orderly and disciplined. They *never* ran away from the battlefield.

Fighting a battle

1 The Roman army lined up like this:

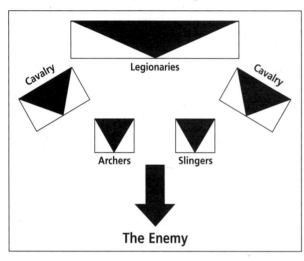

2 Before the battle started, stones and arrows were fired at the enemy.

3 Soldiers marched up close to the enemy and threw their javelins.

4 Soldiers then charged using their swords and shields.

Attacking forts

The Romans were very good at smashing down the walls of forts.

They had excellent weapons and ways for doing this.

1 Catapults

Small catapults fired arrows with a sharp metal point.

Large catapults fired stones. Some of these stones were huge. One soldier had his head knocked off by a big stone. His head landed over 500 metres away!

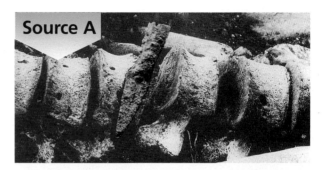

Source A

This person was killed by an arrow fired by a catapult. You can still see the arrowhead in his spine!

2 Battering rams

These were used to break down walls. They were made from huge tree trunks, with a large metal point at the end.

3 The tortoise formation

Often the Romans joined shields above their heads to form a shape like a tortoise. The shields protected the men from arrows and spears fired at their heads.

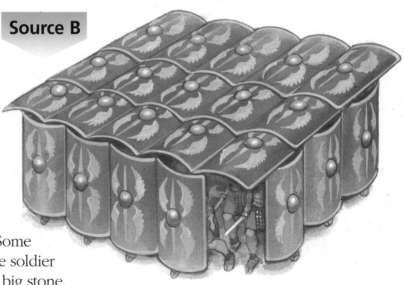

Source B

A group of soldiers in a tortoise formation.

4 Siege towers

These were made of wood. They were pushed up to the walls of the fort. From the top soldiers threw javelins at the enemy. They then climbed over the wall.

Roman soldiers attack a fort from inside a siege tower. Note the arrows being shot from the top, and the battering ram at the bottom of the tower.

Source C

The army had plenty of work to do in peacetime.

Army work

- Many hours were spent training and doing boring jobs (see Source A).
- When the army moved, the soldiers had to build a new camp.
- When a new country was conquered, the soldiers had to build forts.

Building work

- The army built many miles of road. The roads were straight and had cobblestones on top.

Source A

A list of jobs done by Roman soldiers in peacetime.

- **Digging ditches**
- **Cleaning the barracks**
- **Cleaning boots**
- **Mending weapons.**

How a Roman road was made

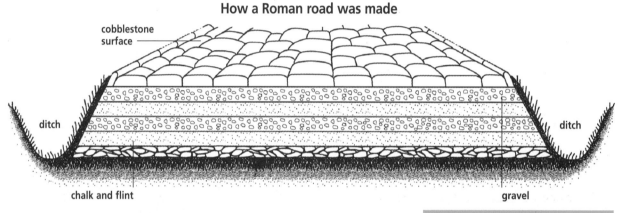

cobblestone surface

ditch

ditch

chalk and flint

gravel

- The army built Hadrian's Wall, which stretched across northern Britain.

A Roman carving showing soldiers building a fort.

Source B

Fun and games

When they were not working, the soldiers had to make their own fun and amusements. They liked gambling games. They played dice and a form of noughts and crosses. Board games were also very popular (Source D).

Source C

From a letter to a Roman soldier. It was found at the fort of Vindolanda in Northumberland.

I have sent you some socks, two pairs of sandals and two pairs of underpants. I wish you the best of luck.

Source D

From *The Times* newspaper, 25 September 1996.

ROMAN BOARD GAME FOUND

A board game played by the Romans has been found in a grave in Essex. The grave is 2,000 years old.

The game was found next to the bones of its owner. It had been buried with the owner so that he could have some fun in the afterlife. The pieces are laid out ready to play.

The excited archaeologist said:

'We found a whole row of blue pieces. Then we found the white pieces. It was like magic. Bits of the playing board are there too. The wooden bits of the board have rotted away, but the metal edges are still there.'

Glass beads

Hinge

55 cm

Wooden board

40 cm

Questions

1 Look at pages 26–7.
  Write down four things the Romans used to attack forts.

2 Read **Building work** on page 28.
  What two kinds of building work did the army do?

3 Look at page 29.
  How do we know that the Romans played board games?

29

The Republic

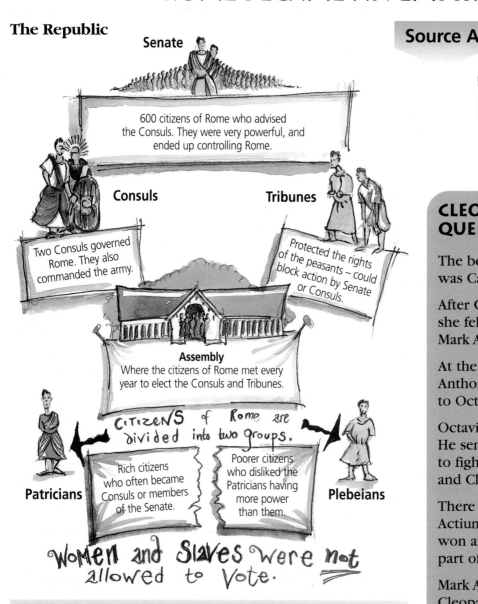

Senate

600 citizens of Rome who advised the Consuls. They were very powerful, and ended up controlling Rome.

Consuls

Two Consuls governed Rome. They also commanded the army.

Tribunes

Protected the rights of the peasants – could block action by Senate or Consuls.

Assembly

Where the citizens of Rome met every year to elect the Consuls and Tribunes.

CITIZENS of Rome are divided into two groups.

Patricians

Rich citizens who often became Consuls or members of the Senate.

Plebeians

Poorer citizens who disliked the Patricians having more power than them.

WOMEN and SLAVES were not allowed to vote.

Rome was ruled by kings until 509 BC. After that Rome was a republic. A republic does not have a king. This is how the republic worked.

The Republic breaks down

By 100 BC the army had become very powerful. The Senate could not control the army. Some generals in the army wanted to get power.

They began fighting each other to see who could rule Rome. The most famous general who wanted to rule Rome was **Julius Caesar**.

Source A

CLEOPATRA – QUEEN OF EGYPT

The beautiful Cleopatra was Caesar's lover.

After Caesar's death, she fell in love with Mark Anthony in 41 BC.

At the time Mark Anthony was married to Octavian's sister.

Octavian was angry. He sent an army to Egypt to fight Mark Anthony and Cleopatra.

There was a sea battle at Actium in 31 BC. Octavian won and he made Egypt part of the Roman Empire.

Mark Anthony and Cleopatra then killed themselves.

Cleopatra was said to have put a snake on her chest. The snake gave her a poisonous bite.

Who was Julius Caesar?

Caesar was born in 100 BC. He came from a rich family. He was clever and good at sport. He was made a **Consul** in 59 BC, and then was put in charge of the Roman army in Gaul.

A coin with Caesar's head on it. The words mean 'Caesar dictator for life'.

Dictator for life

Caesar was a brilliant general. He beat the Gauls in battle many times and won more land for Rome. This made him very popular. He went back to Rome and was loudly cheered by the people.

Caesar was made dictator (ruler) for life. He was now the most powerful man in Rome.

Murder!

Some people in the Senate did not like Caesar. They thought he had too much power. They decided to murder him. On 15 March 44 BC, Caesar was stabbed to death in the Senate House. A Roman writer told how horrible it was:

> *A group of men crowded round Caesar. One held his shoulders and another stabbed him in the throat. He was stabbed 23 more times. Caesar was left lying dead. Then three of his slaves carried him home.*

A contest for power

After this there was a contest between **Mark Anthony**, **Octavian** and **Lepidus** to see who should rule the Empire. Octavian won.

The first emperor

In 27 BC Octavian became the first emperor. The republic had ended. Octavian now called himself **Augustus**, which means 'respected one'. The cartoon on pages 32–33 tells you more about these events.

How much power did the emperors have?

From 27 BC Rome was ruled by an emperor.

The emperor was very powerful:

1 The emperor was in charge of the army.

2 The emperor picked the people to run the city of Rome.

3 The emperor picked the people to run the Empire.

4 The emperor was in charge of the money. He often spent it on such things as:

- gladiator fights
- free bread for the people
- higher wages for the army.

This made him popular and kept him in power.

509 BC Tarquinius Superbus, the last King of Rome, was driven out. Rome became a republic.

In 107 BC the Consul Marius opened up the army to all citizens. The army became too big for the Consuls and Senate to control.

27 BC Octavian was made Rome's first emperor, taking the name Augustus Caesar.

Mark Anthony fell in love with Cleopatra, the Queen of Egypt. He was married to Octavian's sister at the time. This made Octavian very angry.

In 31 BC Octavian defeated Mark Anthony in battle. Mark Anthony and Cleopatra committed suicide.

Julius Caesar was made Consul in 59 BC and put in charge of the Roman army in Gaul. He returned in 49 BC having beaten all the tribes of Gaul. Caesar started acting like a king. In 44 BC a group of Senators tried to save the republic by murdering Caesar.

Questions

1 Look at the cartoon.
  Copy these sentences. Fill in the gaps.

  a The last _____ was driven out in 509 BC.
  b Rome then became a _____.

2 Who became the first Roman emperor in 27 BC?

Disaster strikes Pompeii

Pompeii was a town in southern Italy. It was built near a volcano called Mount Vesuvius. The volcano had been quiet for hundreds of years.

Suddenly, on 24 August AD 79, the volcano blew up. The top of the volcano was blown hundreds of metres into the air. Ash and hot rocks fell on to the terrified people of Pompeii.

Poisonous gas

Many people were choked by poisonous gases and fumes from the volcano.

They could not breathe. They dropped to the ground and died.

Soon their bodies were covered under six metres of hot ashes.

Source A

The ruins of Pompeii. This was painted by an English artist in 1820.

Source B

An eye-witness tells what happened at Pompeii. He was writing many years later.

There was total darkness.

You could hear people shouting and screaming.

Parents called out for their children.

Children called out for their parents.

People thought it was the end of the world.

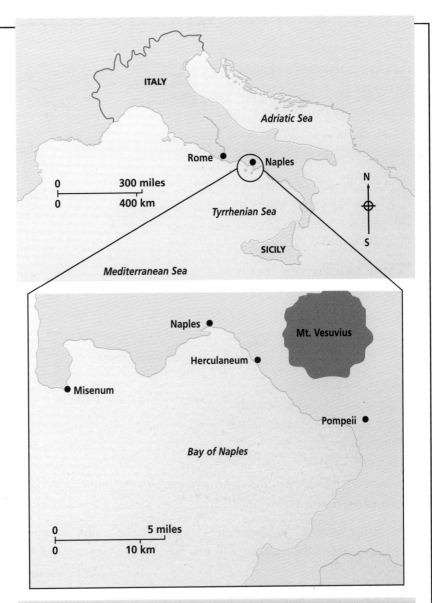

Pompeii and the Bay of Naples. Mount Vesuvius was very close.

Panic

There was panic as people tried to escape.

Some people tried to escape in boats. But the sea was very rough. Skeletons have been found near the water's edge.

Historians think the boats capsized and people were drowned.

Not many horse skeletons have been found at Pompeii. So it seems possible that some people rode to safety on horseback.

A terrible death

Pompeii was buried under a huge pile of ash and rocks. Thousands of men, women and children died a terrible death.

Archaeologists dig up Pompeii

Pompeii lay buried for 1,700 years. All that could be seen was a large mound of earth.

Archaeologists wanted to know what lay under the earth. So they began digging.

What buildings have been found?

By carefully digging up the ground, archaeologists have found:

- the town wall
- streets laid out in a grid
- the **forum** (market place)
- bath-houses
- two theatres
- a sports field with a swimming pool
- an **amphitheatre** (stadium).

The things found at Pompeii tell us a lot about how the Romans lived.

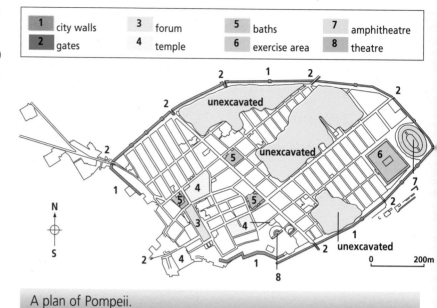

1 city walls		**3** forum		**5** baths		**7** amphitheatre	
2 gates		**4** temple		**6** exercise area		**8** theatre	

A plan of Pompeii.

Plaster-cast models of the dead

Archaeologists found signs of many dead bodies – people and animals. But their flesh had rotted away and left holes in the ash. Each hole was the same shape as a dead body.

The archaeologists poured liquid plaster into the holes. When the plaster went hard, it made a plaster-cast model of the dead body (see Sources C and D). A lot of these plaster-cast models have been made.

How big was Pompeii?

Archaeologists think that about 20,000 people lived in Pompeii.

The town covered an area of 64 hectares. The plan (above) shows you how the streets were laid out.

Source C

The body of a person who died in a street.

A loaf of bread from Pompeii. It looks perfect, but is rock hard!

Source D

The body of a dog found at Pompeii. It had been chained up. It died trying to get free.

Last moments

Here are some of the dead people found at Pompeii. Archaeologists can tell what they were doing at the very moment they died.

- A beggar with a new pair of shoes found on a street corner
- Eighteen people huddled together in a cellar
- A woman with some fine jewels
- Two prisoners chained up in a cell
- Seven children killed when a baker's house fell on them.

Questions

1 Read **Disaster strikes Pompeii** on page 34.

   a Which volcano was near to Pompeii?

   b Write a sentence to say what happened in AD 79.

   c What fell on to the people?

2 Read **Poisonous gas** on page 34.

   How did the gas kill people?

3 Read Source B on page 35.

   Would you trust what this person tells us?

4 Look at pages 36 and 37.

   a Make a list of things that the archaeologists found at Pompeii.

   b Why are these things important to us today?

Chariot racing

The Romans loved to have a day out at the chariot racing.

In Rome there was a big race track called the Circus Maximus.

It could hold about 250,000 people.

The races

There could be as many as twelve chariots in a race.

Each chariot was pulled by four horses. They did seven laps of the track, a distance of eight kilometres.

The racing was dangerous. There were many crashes. The drivers were often injured and some were even killed.

The crowd

The drivers wore different team colours. People had banners to show which driver they supported. They gambled lots of money on who would win the races.

The drivers

The best drivers were paid a lot of money.

Many drivers were slaves. If they earned a lot of money, they would buy their freedom.

The Games

In Rome there was another large stadium called the Colosseum. It was here that the Games were held.

Source A

A scene from a modern film called *Ben Hur*. It shows a chariot race.

Source B

This Roman did not like chariot races.

I am not interested in the races. Once you have seen one race, you have seen them all.

People only go to see the drivers' colours. They do not go to see the skill of the drivers or the speed of the horses.

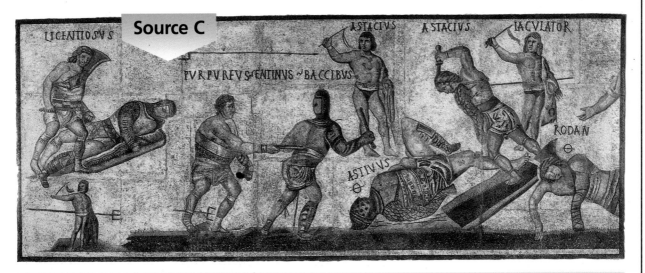

Source C

LICENTIOSVS   PVRPVREVS CENTINVS ~BACCIBVS   ASTACIVS   A STACIVS   IACVLATOR   ASTIVVS   RODAN

A Roman mosaic showing gladiators fighting.

The Games were made up of different things such as:

1 Animals doing tricks.

2 Hungry animals fighting to the death.

3 Animals being hunted in the arena and then killed.

4 Criminals fighting lions and tigers. The criminals did not have any weapons and were usually killed.

Gladiator fights

Gladiators were slaves, prisoners of war or criminals. They were trained to fight to the death.

If a gladiator was wounded, he raised his finger. This showed that he was asking for mercy.

If he had fought well, he was allowed to live. If he had fought badly, he was killed by the other gladiator. Most fights ended in death.

Source D

This Roman did not like the Games.

All I saw was murder. The fights are cruel and always end in death.

The crowd is very bloodthirsty. People shout out: 'Kill him! Beat him! Burn him! What a coward he is!'

Questions

1 Read **Chariot racing** and **The Games**. Copy these sentences. Fill in the gaps.

  a Chariot racing was held at the _____ _____.
  b The Games were held at the _____.

2 Read **Gladiator fights**.

  a What did a gladiator do to show he wanted mercy?
  b What happened if he had fought well?
  c What happened if he had fought badly?

3 Read Source D.
  'All Romans were cruel and bloodthirsty.'
  Is this statement true or false?

What was a villa?

A villa was a big house in the countryside. Only rich Romans lived in villas. Many villas were on a farm.

Inside a villa

Most villas had lots of rooms. There were beautiful paintings on the walls. There were **mosaics** on the floor. Mosaics were made up of lots of tiny pieces of coloured stone. They were made into a pattern.

Many villas had a **hypocaust**. This was a type of central heating.

Meals

The villa owner was rich. He and his family lived a good life. They ate three meals a day:

1 **Breakfast**: A light snack of bread and honey.

2 **Mid-morning snack**: Bread and cheese.

3 **Dinner**: This was the main meal of the day. It was eaten in the late afternoon.

People laid on couches to eat the food. They did not use knives and forks. Instead, they ate with their fingers!

If the owner had guests, the meal would be eight courses. Dishes such as pheasant, partridge and stuffed dormouse were served.

If they were full, people left the room and made themselves sick. Then they carried on eating!

Ordinary people in the countryside

We do not know much about ordinary Romans. Not much was written about them. Most of their houses have rotted away.

Houses

Most ordinary people in the countryside lived in small, round houses with a thatched roof. The roof had a hole in it for the smoke to get out. The floor was made of beaten earth.

Meals

Ordinary country people ate porridge made from wheat. Spices and vegetables were put into the porridge. This gave it more flavour.

These people did not eat fish or meat very often. Meat was very dear.

Questions

1 Read **What was a villa?**
Copy these sentences. Fill in the gaps.

A villa was _____.
Only _____ _____ lived in villas.

2 Read **Inside a villa**.

a What would be seen on the walls?
b What would be seen on the floor?
c What was a hypocaust?

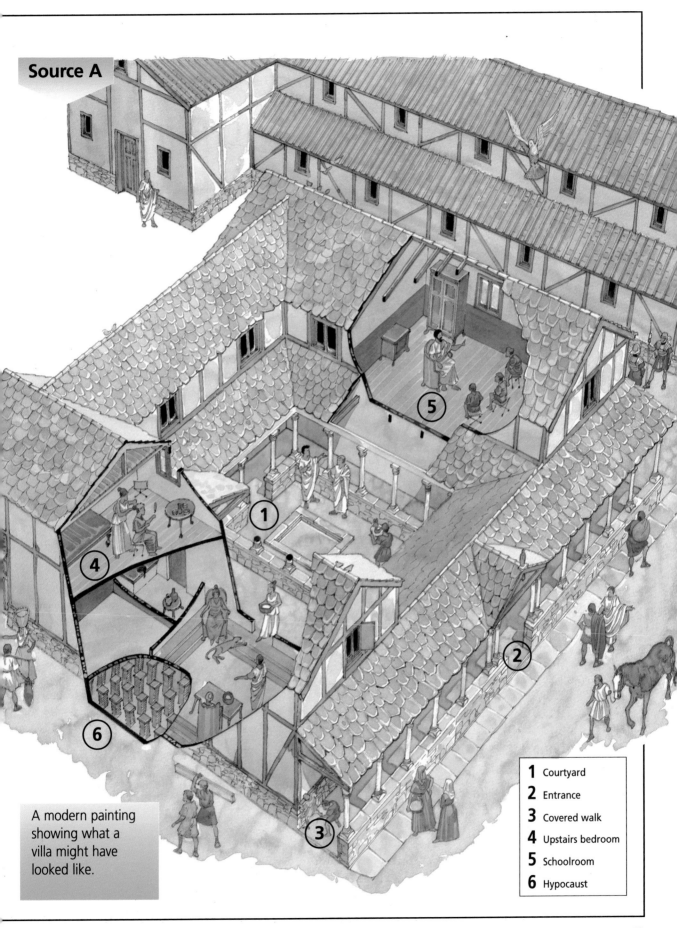

A modern painting showing what a villa might have looked like.

1 Courtyard
2 Entrance
3 Covered walk
4 Upstairs bedroom
5 Schoolroom
6 Hypocaust

Roman villas had their own baths. Baths had a lot of rooms. Each room had a different purpose. The Romans really enjoyed having a bath.

4 They went into the hot steam room. The bathers rubbed perfumed oil on their skin. As they sweated, they took off the oil with a scraper called a **strigil**.

Source A

5 Finally they plunged into a cold bath.

1 The bathers took off their clothes. They put sandals on so they would not burn their feet.

2 The bathers did some exercises.

A modern painting of a Roman bath-house. You can see the hypocaust furnace outside the main building.

3 They went into the warm room.

Keeping tidy – men

Rich men were clean shaven. Their faces were shaved by a slave or they went to a barber. Poor men could not afford to go to a barber. So they usually had a beard.

Many men were scared of going bald. They rubbed in potions which they thought would stop their hair falling out. One potion was made of rat droppings!

Keeping tidy – women

Women often changed the style of their hair. Some wore wigs to look good. They wore face creams made from milk and flour. They also wore scent which came from India.

Question

Are these statements **true** or **false**?

- The Romans were dirty people.
- The Romans did not care what they looked like.

Explain your answers.

The ruins of a hypocaust at Chedworth Roman villa.

Source C

An oil can and strigil.

Source D

A Roman complains about his barber.

If you want to stay alive, keep away from Antiochus the barber.

I did not get the scars on my chin from boxing. Nor was I scratched by the sharp nails of an angry wife.

The scars came from the razor of Antiochus.

Source B

Source E

From a Roman poem.

Galla, you get your beauty from the chemist. Your hair is dyed with German herbs. You have false teeth which you keep in a box – just like your dresses.

45

A Roman family

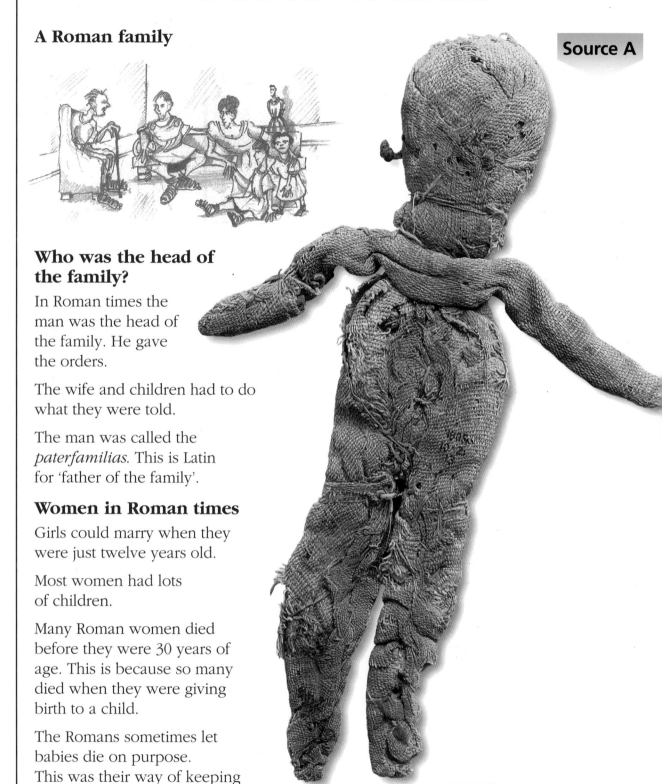

Source A

Who was the head of the family?

In Roman times the man was the head of the family. He gave the orders.

The wife and children had to do what they were told.

The man was called the *paterfamilias*. This is Latin for 'father of the family'.

Women in Roman times

Girls could marry when they were just twelve years old.

Most women had lots of children.

Many Roman women died before they were 30 years of age. This is because so many died when they were giving birth to a child.

The Romans sometimes let babies die on purpose. This was their way of keeping the population down (see Source B).

Roman children played with similar toys to us. This rag doll, from Roman times, was found in Egypt.

Poor children

Children from poor homes had a hard life. They were sent out to work at an early age. Some poor children were sold as slaves to rich families.

Rich children

Children from rich homes had a good life. They had lots of toys to play with. Archaeologists have found dolls' houses, rocking horses and rag dolls.

Girls were taught to be housewives. Boys spent time running and throwing spears. This would later help them to get into the Roman army.

Schools

Rich children started school when they were seven. The teachers were strict. They often used the cane.

Lessons lasted from dawn until noon. The same teacher taught all subjects.

Just like today the children were taught reading, writing and arithmetic.

Poor children did not go to school. They grew up unable to read and write.

Source B

MASS BABIES' GRAVE FOUND IN ISRAEL

Scientists have found a mass grave of over 100 babies in Israel. They think the grave was dug in the 4th century AD. Israel was then part of the Roman Empire.

The babies were only one or two days old.

A scientist said: 'It was normal in Roman time to let babies die. They did it to keep the population down.'

From the *Guardian* newspaper, 16 January 1997.

Questions

1 Read Source B.

    a Where was the grave found?
    b How many dead babies were in it?
    c How old were the babies when they died?
    d Why had the babies been allowed to die by the Romans?

2 Read **Poor children** and **Rich children**.

    a What was life like for poor children?
    b What was life like for rich children?

3 Read **Schools**.
Make a list of how Roman schools were different from schools today.

Large numbers of slaves

There were over 400,000 slaves in Rome. Only rich people had slaves. The poor could not afford slaves.

Slave markets

When the Romans captured a country, they took many prisoners. The prisoners were taken to Rome. Here they were sold to be slaves.

People would bid money to buy the slaves. It was rather like buying furniture or an animal!

What work did slaves do?

Strong men worked on farms or built roads

Clever people worked as doctors or teachers

Others worked as maids, gardeners and cooks

Source A

A Roman mosaic of a boy slave.

Life as a slave

Some slaves were treated badly. Others had a better life than if they had been free.

Slaves who ran away were punished. If a slave murdered his owner, all the other slaves in the house were put to death.

Slaves who worked hard were often given their freedom. They could then buy land, but they were not allowed to vote.

Source B

A nobleman praises another Roman for being kind to his slaves.

I have **heard you are kind to your slaves. I am pleased about this. They may be slaves, but they are also humans as well.**

A statue of the Roman god Mars.

Some Roman gods

Jupiter: The king of the gods
Juno: The queen of the gods
Mars: The god of war
Mercury: The messenger of the gods
Neptune: The god of the sea
Venus: The goddess of love

The emperor said it was against the law to be a Christian.

Christians were forced to pray in secret. If the Romans found out, the Christians were cruelly treated.

Many Christians were killed when they were made to fight wild animals in the Colosseum. Most Romans thought this was good fun!

Christianity allowed in Rome

In AD 324 **Emperor Constantine** became a Christian. Many Romans copied him.

In AD 380 Christianity became the main religion of the Empire. Other religions were not allowed after this.

Many gods

The Romans had lots of different gods. They built temples to their gods.

Gifts and sacrifices

There were festivals on special days for each god.

People wanted to please the gods. So they gave gifts of flowers and fruit to the gods. They sometimes killed an animal as a **sacrifice**.

Cruel treatment of Christians

Some people in the Roman Empire became Christians.

Christians did not believe in the Roman gods. They believed in Jesus Christ.

Questions

1 What kinds of job did slaves do?

2 Copy this sentence. Fill in the gaps. Use the words in the box.

At first the Romans had _____ _____, but they later became _____.

| Christians | Many gods |

7.1 ROMAN BRITAIN

Julius Caesar

Julius Caesar was in charge of the Roman army in Gaul (modern-day France).

Why did Caesar invade Britain?

He was angry that the British had helped the Gauls to fight the Romans.

He wanted the gold, silver and tin in Britain.

He would be liked in Rome if he beat the British.

Caesar lands in Kent, 55 BC

Caesar's small army arrived in Kent in 55 BC.

The British were waiting for them on the beach. They had spears and looked very fierce. At first the Romans were too frightened to get out of their boats (see Source B).

When they finally landed, the Romans marched a few miles inland. They took some prisoners.

Then a storm damaged their ships. The Romans mended the ships and sailed back to Gaul.

Caesar returns to Britain, 54 BC

Caesar went back to Britain in 54 BC. This time he had a bigger army. He marched further inland and beat the British in a battle. Caesar captured some prisoners and took money from the British.

But Caesar was worried that there would a rebellion in Gaul while he was away. So he decided to go back to Gaul.

It was to be almost 100 years before the Romans invaded Britain again.

Source A

A modern painting of Julius Caesar's invasion of Britain in 55 BC.

Source B

Caesar tells what happened when he came to Britain in 55 BC.

My soldiers were not used to landing from boats and paddling on to a beach.

They did not want to get out of the boats.

The British threw spears and galloped into the sea.

Then our standard-bearer shouted: 'Do you want us to lose our eagle?'

He jumped out of the boat and walked towards the British. The other soldiers followed him.

Questions

1 Read **Why did Caesar invade Britain?**
Write down one reason why Caesar went to Britain.

2 Copy these sentences. Fill in the gaps. Use the words in the box.

Caesar first went to Britain in _____.
He went back _____ year later in _____.

54 BC	one	55 BC

3 Read Source B.
Why do you think the Romans were frightened to land?

Why did the Romans invade Britain in AD 43?

In AD 43 the **Emperor Claudius** ordered the Roman army to invade Britain again. Why did he do this?

1 He wanted Britain to be part of the Roman Empire.
2 He wanted to show people he was strong.
3 He was angry with the British for helping the Gauls.

Demons!

The Roman soldiers did not want to invade Britain. They thought they would sail off the edge of the world. Stories went round that Britain was a land full of demons. The soldiers had to be talked into getting off the ships.

The Romans arrive in Britain

A Roman army of 40,000 men finally landed in Kent.

The British put up a good fight. Their leader was **Caractacus**. He was beaten by the Romans in a battle near the river Medway. Caractacus fled to Wales.

The Romans then captured Colchester. Claudius was very pleased. His two-year-old son was renamed Britannicus.

Source A

A speech made in Rome by Caractacus. After the speech he was allowed to live.

If I had not put up such a good fight, your victory would not look so great.

If you kill me, you will look very cruel.

If you let me live, people will say that the Romans are kind and can show mercy.

THE HEAD OF CLAUDIUS

In 1907, a boy swimming in a river in Suffolk spotted something on the river bed.

He dived down to see what it was, and pulled out this bronze head of Claudius!

It is now in the British Museum, London.

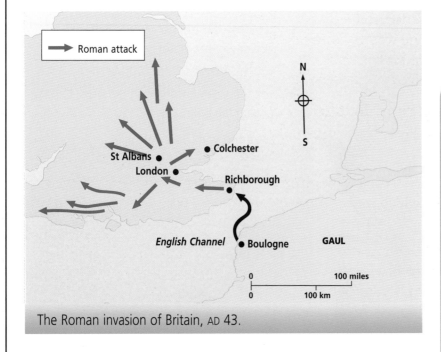

The Roman invasion of Britain, AD 43.

Maiden Castle in Dorset. This was a British fort. It was captured by the Romans.

Caractacus is captured

The Romans captured Caractacus. He was tied up and taken to Rome. He was paraded in the streets and made fun of. Claudius said he was going to kill Caractacus. But Caractacus made such a brave speech that he was allowed to live (see Source A).

The Romans conquer more of Britain

The Romans soon had the east and south of Britain under control.

But it took longer to conquer the west and north of Britain. The land there is hilly, which makes it hard for fighting.

Emperor Hadrian decided to build a wall to protect the land that the Romans had captured. Hadrian's Wall was the northern border of the Roman Empire.

Questions

1 Look at page 52.

  a Who ordered the invasion of Britain in AD 43?

  b Who was the British leader?

  c Which town did the Romans capture?

2 Read **The Romans conquer more of Britain**.

  a Which part of Britain was conquered quickly?

  b Why was it harder for the Romans to conquer the west and north of Britain?

Source A

Hadrian's Wall today.

Why was Hadrian's Wall built?

In AD 117, tribes from Scotland and the north of England attacked the Romans. They caused a lot of damage.

The Emperor Hadrian was worried. So he visited Britain. He saw that it would be very hard to conquer the Scots.

Hadrian decided to build a wall to keep the Scots out. The wall was built between Wallsend-on-Tyne and Bowness-on-Solway. It was 117 kilometres long.

Building the wall

It took thousands of soldiers five years to build the wall.

Success

The wall did its job well. It stopped the Scots from attacking. The wall was so well built that parts of it are still standing today (see Source A).

The five parts of the wall

1 The wall was 6 metres tall and 3 metres wide. It was built out of stone.

2 On the north side of the wall a huge ditch was dug. Attackers would have to cross this ditch before they got to the wall.

3 There was another ditch, or **vallum**, on the south side of the wall. This was not so deep. The Romans did not expect to be attacked from the south.

4 There was a fort every eight kilometres along the wall. Each fort had 500 soldiers. The forts also had workshops, food stores, barracks and a hospital.

5 Between the forts were **milecastles**. They held 100 men. Between the milecastles were **turrets**. These had two or three soldiers on watch. They would signal the forts if an attack was about to happen.

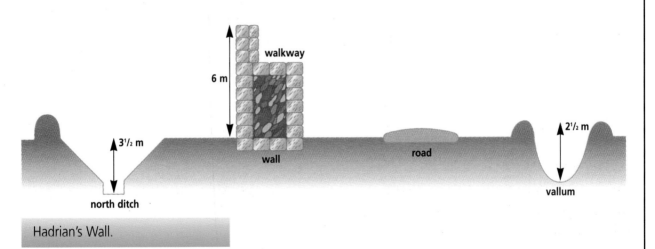

Hadrian's Wall.

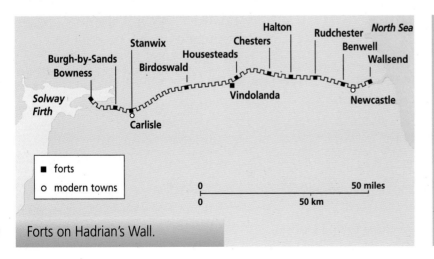

Forts on Hadrian's Wall.

Questions

1 Read **Why was Hadrian's Wall built?**

   a Write down a reason why the wall was built.

   b How long was the wall?

2 What can we learn from Source A about Hadrian's Wall?

About Vindolanda

Vindolanda was a Roman fort near Hadrian's Wall.

In the 1970s, archaeologists dug up the fort. They found many interesting things which tell us a lot about the Romans.

The Vindolanda tablets

The archaeologists were very excited to find bits of wood called **tablets**. The tablets have writing on them.

Some of the tablets have rotted, but it is still possible to work out what they say.

The tablets tell us about life in the Roman army. Some are letters home from soldiers living in the fort.

The tablets are important because we have little else to tell us about ordinary Roman people.

Source A

A model of what a Roman kitchen may have looked like.

Source B

A list of food and drink from the Vindolanda tablets.

Wine, garlic, fish, pork, cereal, butter, deer, beer, spices, beans, goat, barley, lentils, honey, olives, oysters, eggs, bread, ham, plums, chicken, radishes, salt, pepper, semolina.

Source C

The ruined buildings at Vindolanda.

Source D

A pendant found at Vindolanda.

Source E

A child's sandal found at Vindolanda.

Source F

Writing from the Vindolanda tablets.

1 FROM CLAUDIA SEVERA TO SULPICIA LEPIDINA

I send greetings to Lepidina. It is my birthday. Make sure you come to see me, so the day will be more enjoyable.

2 A CALL FOR MERCY

I beg your majesty not to let me be beaten with a stick. I am innocent. I have done nothing wrong.

3 FROM SOLEMIS TO HIS BROTHER, PARIS

I send you greetings. I am very well. I hope you are well, too. You are very bad at writing. You have not sent me one single letter. I am a kinder person, so I am writing this letter to you.

Questions

1 Read **About Vindolanda** on page 58.

   a What was Vindolanda?
   b Where was Vindolanda?

2 Read **The Vindolanda tablets** on page 58.

   a What were the tablets made of?
   b What did they have on them?
   c What do the tablets tell us about?
   d Why are they important to us?

3 Look at Sources C, D and E.
   What does each source tell us about the Romans?

8.1 THE ROMANS: GONE, BUT NOT FORGOTTEN

The end of the Roman Empire

The Roman Empire collapsed when it was attacked by fierce **barbarian** tribes.

By AD 476 the Roman Empire was at an end.

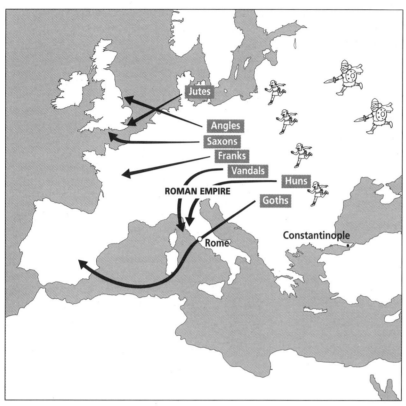

Barbarian tribes attacked the Empire from all directions.

English words which come from Latin words

English	Latin
Navy	*Navis* (a ship)
Video	*Video* (I see)
Science	*Scio* (I know)

Roman numerals are still used today. For example, on clocks.

The Arch of Titus. It was built by the Romans in AD 81.

What have the Romans left us?

Although the Empire came to an end, a lot of Roman things have lived on right up to today.

1 The Latin language

The Romans spoke Latin. Many modern English words come from Latin words (see box).

Coats of arms and badges have Latin sayings on them. Latin is still taught in some of our schools. Flowers and plants all have Latin names.

Source A

2 Books and art

The Romans wrote many plays, stories and poems. They also wrote history books. We still have many of these books.

The Romans were very good at making statues and carvings. Later artists have copied the Roman way of carving statues.

3 The Christian religion

The Romans became Christians. Christianity is still the main religion in countries which used to be in the Roman Empire, such as Britain, Spain, France and Italy.

The Pope still lives in Rome. He is the head of the Roman Catholic Church.

4 Buildings

Many Roman buildings were very grand. They were so well built that some are still standing.

- Much of the Colosseum in Rome is still standing.
- Parts of Hadrian's Wall can still be seen.
- Some Roman roads are still in use. The modern A1 was once a Roman road called Ermine Street. It is a very straight road.

Many later builders copied the Roman way of building (see Source B).

Conclusion

The Romans controlled large parts of Europe, North Africa and the Middle East. It is here that Roman things have been left behind. So in these parts of the world the Romans have not been forgotten.

But we must also remember that millions of other people in the world never saw a Roman. If you go to South America, Japan or Australia you will not see any old Roman buildings.

Source B

The Arc de Triomphe in Paris, built in 1806–36. You can see how the French have copied the Romans.

Questions

1 Read **The end of the Roman Empire**. Why did the Roman Empire end?

2 Look at the numbered sub-headings on these pages. Make a list of things the Romans have left us.

61

The Romans leave Britain

In AD 410 the Roman army left Britain. It went back to Rome to fight off the barbarian tribes.

The Anglo-Saxons

The Anglo-Saxons were next to invade Britain. They came from Germany and Denmark. The British fled westwards to escape the Anglo-Saxons.

The Anglo-Saxons built villages in the south and east of England. They lived in wooden huts and farmed the land. The towns left by the Romans fell down.

Seven kingdoms

By AD 600 the Anglo-Saxons controlled most of England.

The Anglo-Saxons divided England into seven kingdoms. Each kingdom had its own king. The three most important kingdoms were:

- Wessex
- Mercia
- Northumbria.

The Saxon kingdoms often fought each other.

At first the Anglo-Saxons prayed to lots of gods. But they later became Christians.

Source B

This is a page from a bible made by Anglo-Saxon monks at Lindisfarne.

When the Vikings attacked Lindisfarne the monks saved the bible.

Source A

What an Anglo-Saxon monk said about the Vikings in AD 793.

Vikings were savages. They robbed and killed monks, priests and animals.

They attacked Lindisfarne and stole treasure from the church. They killed many monks. Other monks were taken away in chains or drowned in the sea.

Alfred the Great was the King of Wessex from 871 to 899.

The Vikings

The Vikings raided England in 787. They came from Norway, Sweden and Denmark.

The Vikings attacked Saxon villages, killing and stealing. They captured most of eastern England.

Alfred of Wessex

King Alfred of Wessex fought the Vikings (or Danes as they are often called) and won back a lot of the land they had taken. Later Alfred's son was made the king of the whole of England. This stopped the Saxons fighting each other. The Danes kept invading. So many came that they made Danes kings of England.

Were the Vikings savages?

Some people say that the Vikings were wild savages (see Source A).

They robbed and burned down Saxon villages. They also tortured people.

But there was also a peaceful side to the Vikings (see Source D).

Source D

What one Viking said about himself.

I am very good at chess and nine other sports.
I can read and I write poetry.
I can ski, shoot and row.
I can also play the harp.

How was the country run?

1 The king and the Witan

The king ruled the country. He was advised by a council of earls (nobles) called the **Witan**.

The Witan chose the king. They always tried to choose someone who would be strong. But this did not always work out.

2 The earls

The earls were powerful. They had their own armies and owned a lot of land. The ordinary people lived on land owned by the local earl. They had to do what the earl told them.

Edward the Confessor

In 1042 the Witan chose Edward the Confessor to be king.

Edward lived for a time in Normandy in France. Edward was a relation of **William, Duke of Normandy**. The two men were friends.

Earl Godwin

Edward was a weak king and could not keep the earls under control. The strongest earl was **Earl Godwin of Wessex**. He had helped Edward to get the throne. Earl Godwin had a lot of say in running England. Godwin's son was called **Harold Godwinson**.

Edward died in 1066. Both Harold Godwinson and William, Duke of Normandy thought they were going to be the next King of England!

Ordinary people

Most people had to work hard to earn a living. They did not have time to think about who was going to be the next king.

The king and his Witan. The Witan gave advice to the king.

Source E

Ploughing the land. Most ordinary people worked on the land.
Their lives were hard.

Saxon villages

Most people lived in small villages like this one. The houses
were made out of a wooden frame covered with clay and
woven sticks. The lord ran the village.

The Saxons put thieves in the
pillory and stocks.

Saxon towns

Fewer people lived in towns. Villagers went to the nearest
town to sell food, clothes and shoes.

Some people went from town to town selling things.

1066	1100	1150	1200	1250	1300	1350	1400	1450	1500

The medieval period

The twentieth century

1900	1950	2000

The Middle Ages

The Middle Ages lasted for over 400 years.

The Middle Ages started in about 1066 and ended in about 1485.

The phrase 'Middle Ages' has been made up by historians as a label for this time in history.

The Middle Ages are also known as medieval times.

Life in the Middle Ages

- Rich people had lots of time to enjoy themselves (Source A).

- Poor people had to work very hard (Source B and Source C).

- Most people prayed a lot to God (Source D).

Source A

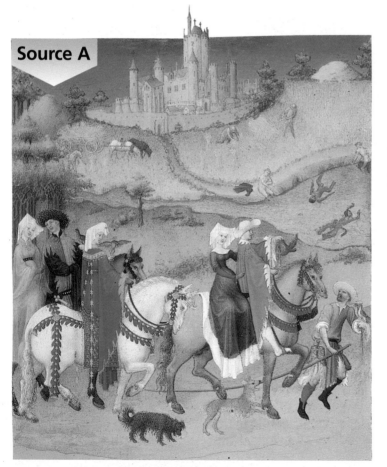

A picture from a book made about 1410. Rich people are out hawking. Hawks were used to kill smaller birds.

Source B

What a medieval person said about poor women.

If the baby cries in the night, the women have to get up and rock the cradle.

They have to darn and wash clothes.

They spin wool to earn more money. But still they have not enough food to feed the children.

The women often go hungry.

Source C

What a medieval person said about life in England.

The lords have a lot of power.

They order the poor people about. The poor people have to:

- plough the lord's fields
- sow and harvest the lord's crops
- carry the crops to the barns
- cut the hay
- gather in wood.

Source D

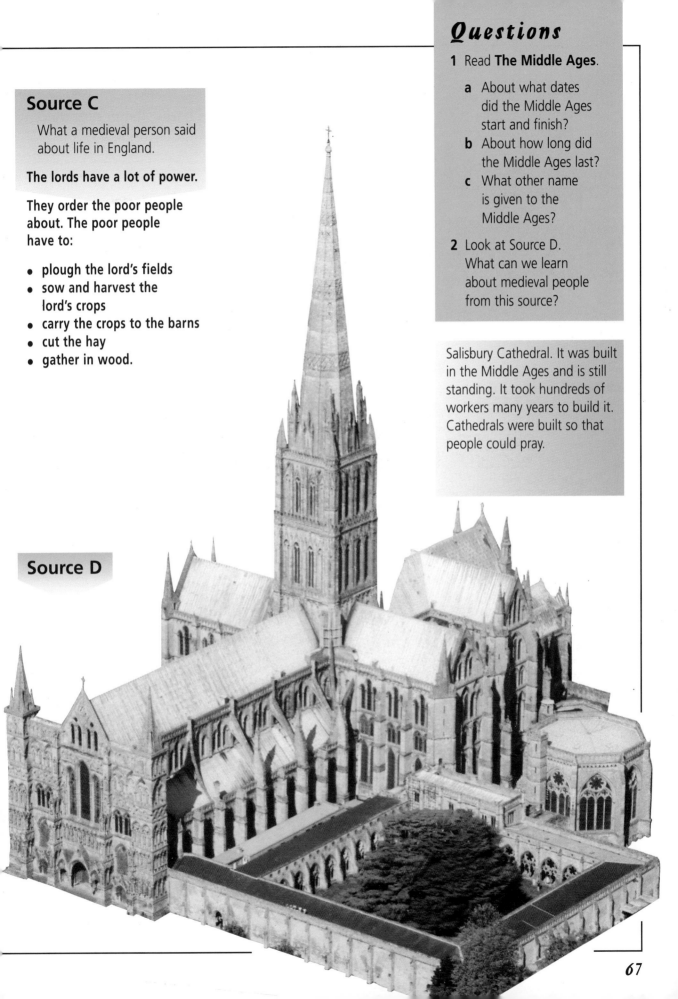

Salisbury Cathedral. It was built in the Middle Ages and is still standing. It took hundreds of workers many years to build it. Cathedrals were built so that people could pray.

Questions

1 Read **The Middle Ages**.

  a About what dates did the Middle Ages start and finish?
  b About how long did the Middle Ages last?
  c What other name is given to the Middle Ages?

2 Look at Source D. What can we learn about medieval people from this source?

67

Who had power in the Middle Ages?

The king ruled England.

The **nobles** also had a lot of power. They were rich enough to have their own armies.

If the king was strong, the country was peaceful.

Henry II (1154–1189) was a strong king. He kept law and order. He controlled the nobles.

If the king ruled badly, the nobles tried to get more say in the running of the country.

King John (1199–1216) was not liked. The nobles argued with him.

They made him sign the **Magna Carta** in 1215, which gave the nobles more power.

Source E

The king and the Church

- The **Pope** was in charge of the Church.

- The Pope lived in Rome.

- He told the bishops and priests in England what to do.

- Sometimes the King of England and the Pope fell out.

A king is crowned. Will this king get on with the Pope?

Wars against France

During the Middle Ages, English kings captured land in France.

The English and the French fought many wars.

The most famous war was the Hundred Years' War. It was fought between 1337 and 1453.

In the end, the English lost nearly all the land they had captured in France.

Heaven and Hell

People believed that bad people went to Hell.

Hell was a place where bad people burned for ever.

People believed that good people went to Heaven.

People thought that God decided who went to Heaven and Hell.

This was why they prayed a lot. They wanted God to think they were good.

Find out more!

This chapter has told you a little about life in the Middle Ages. The rest of this book tells you more about:

- who ruled the country
- town life
- village life
- wars
- the Church.

Read on!

Questions

Look at Source F and read **Heaven and Hell**.

1 What did people in the Middle Ages think Hell was like?

2 Why did people pray a lot?

A painting showing what medieval people thought Hell was like.

Source F

King Edward the Confessor died in 1066. He had no son to become king.

The next king?

Three men wanted to be King of England:

- Harold Godwinson

- Harald Hardrada, King of Norway

- William, Duke of Normandy.

HARALD HARDRADA, KING OF NORWAY

His father was promised the throne by an earlier king

A good fighter

EARL HAROLD GODWINSON

English

Promised the crown by Edward in 1066

A good fighter

NORWAY

N

S

ENGLAND

0   200 miles

0   300 km

NORMANDY

WILLIAM, DUKE OF NORMANDY

Promised the crown by Edward in 1051

He was Edward's cousin

His wife was related to an earlier king

Harold Godwinson had sworn to help William become king

A good fighter

Whom did Edward choose?

Harold   Edward   William

Pictures from the Bayeux Tapestry. The first picture shows Harold promising to help William be king. The second shows King Edward dying. By his bed the English earls are persuading Edward to choose Harold.

Harold as king

Harold was on the spot when King Edward died. He was crowned king. This made William and Harald Hardrada very angry. Harald Hardrada came to England with a big army. But King Harold defeated him in a battle. Now King Harold had to face William.

Source B

September 1066: Harold and William ready to fight.

Questions

1 Read **The next king?**
   Write down the names of the three men who wanted to be king.

2 Look at the picture on page 70.

   a Where did Harald Hardrada come from?
   b Where did William come from?

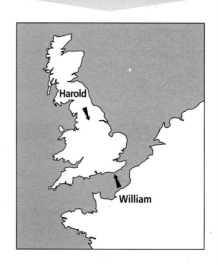

Source A

A modern picture of the Battle of Hastings drawn by Jason Askew this century.

William lands in England

William and his army landed in England in September 1066. They were called **Normans** because they came from Normandy. They marched to Hastings and waited for Harold there.

Harold marches south

Harold was in the north of England when William landed. So he got his army together and marched south to meet William.

On 14 October 1066, Harold reached Hastings. He was ready to fight William.

The Battle of Hastings 1066

Harold set his army up on a hill near Hastings. The hill was called Senlac Hill. William was in the valley below.

The battle begins

At 9 o'clock in the morning, William attacked. The battled raged all day.

Was William dead?

During the battle, someone said William was dead. His soldiers were terrified. But William lifted his helmet. He was all right.

Harold on the hill

Time and again William attacked Harold. But Harold and his soldiers stood firm on top of Senlac Hill.

The end of the battle

Slowly William's soldiers broke through. Harold and his best soldiers were surrounded. Harold's brothers were dead. Soon Harold was dead too. He was hacked to pieces.

Source B

The Bayeux Tapestry is the earliest source about the Battle of Hastings.
It was made between 1076 and 1086.
This picture shows Harold being killed.

William had won

William had won the Battle of Hastings. But could he win all of England?

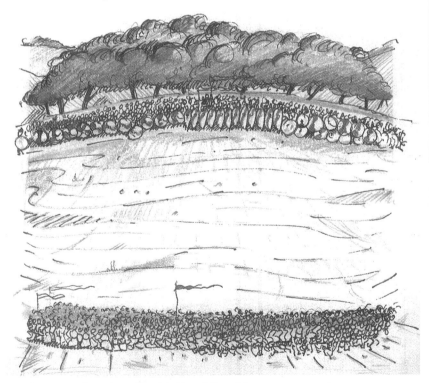

A drawing of Senlac Hill with Harold's soldiers on top and William's soldiers below.

Questions

1 Look at Source B.

   a What is the earliest source about the Battle of Hastings?

   b When was it made between?

   c What does this picture show?

2 Look at Source A.

   a When was it made?

   b Make a list of all the things that are the same in Source A and B. There are at least five.

William is crowned king

William won the Battle of Hastings. He marched to London. He was crowned king on Christmas Day 1066. But William still needed to take control of England.

William burnt villages

William wanted everyone to know he was king. He sent his soldiers into the countryside to make people obey him.

The soldiers burnt people's animals, food and homes. Many people starved to death.

William built castles

William had to make sure that he kept control. He told the Normans to build castles.

These castles dominated the villages around them. They showed people how powerful the Normans were.

William told the Normans to build strong stone castles to dominate the villages.

Source A

The Bayeux Tapestry shows William's soldiers taking villagers' animals in the top picture. They are burning a village in the bottom picture.

William took land from the English

William took land away from the English earls. Any earls who stood against him were killed.

William gave land to the Normans

William gave this land to his Norman friends. But they only kept it as long as they helped William.

William got control of England.

Source B

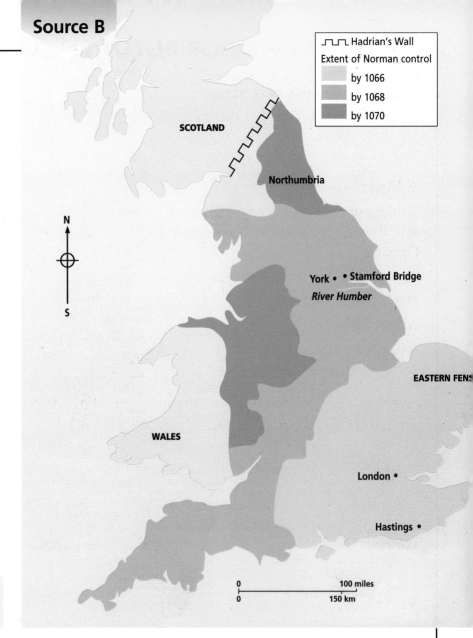

Hadrian's Wall

Extent of Norman control
- by 1066
- by 1068
- by 1070

SCOTLAND

Northumbria

N
S

York • • Stamford Bridge
River Humber

EASTERN FENS

WALES

London •

Hastings •

0   100 miles
0   150 km

DOMVS·IN CEN DITVR·

Questions

1 Read **William is crowned king**.
 When was William crowned king?

2 Look at Source A.

 a What are William's soldiers doing in the top picture?
 b What are William's soldiers doing in the bottom picture?

2.4 A NEW WAY OF RULING?

Ruling England before 1066

Earls were powerful men. They owned a lot of land and helped the king to rule.

After 1066

William did not trust the earls. He took away their land.

William said he owned all the land. He gave it to his Norman friends. But he could take it back too.

The Domesday Book

William wanted to know what England was worth. In 1085 he sent men to every village. They asked:

- the name of the village
- how much land it had
- how many people lived there
- how many ploughs it had
- how many mills it had.

The answers were made into a book called the **Domesday Book**.

Source A

William took land from an English earl. Here William is giving it to his own son-in-law, Alan. Alan is swearing to help William.

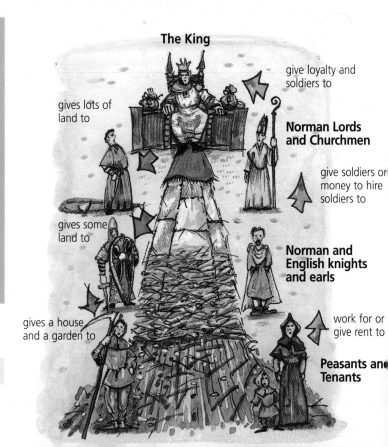

The King

gives lots of land to

give loyalty and soldiers to

Norman Lords and Churchmen

give soldiers or money to hire soldiers to

gives some land to

Norman and English knights and earls

gives a house and a garden to

work for or give rent to

Peasants and Tenants

How the **feudal system** worked. ▶

WALTHEOF THE ENGLISH EARL

Waltheof was an English earl. He fought William fiercely, but William won. Then Waltheof swore to help William.

Waltheof was a good soldier. So William was pleased. William gave his niece, Judith, to Waltheof as a wife.

But Waltheof plotted against William again. William was furious and threw Waltheof into prison. Waltheof swore that he was innocent. Then the Vikings invaded in 1075.

Waltheof's wife said that he had told the Vikings to invade. William had had enough. He had Waltheof beheaded in 1076.

Who did William give the good jobs to?

This is a list of some of the bishops of Winchester. The word 'de' shows that the name is Norman. Richard is also a Norman name.

1007   Brithwold

1015   Elfsimus

1032   Alfwine

1047   Stigand

1070   Walkin

1100   William de Giffard

1129   Henry de Blois

1174   Richard Tocliffe

1189   Godfrey de Lucy

1205   Peter de Rupibus

1243   William de Raleigh

Questions

1 Read **After 1066**.

   a Did William trust the earls?
   b What did he take away from them?
   c What did William say?

2 Read **Who did William give the good jobs to?**
   Write down the date of the first Norman Bishop of Winchester.

How do we know?

There are no early Norman castles left now. So how do we know what a Norman castle looked like? Here are some of the ways:

- the Bayeux Tapestry
- other pictures from Norman times
- books from Norman times
- bits of castles dug up from the ground.

Source B

A monk wrote this description of a castle around 1100.

The castle is on top of a big hill.

From the castle you can keep watch over all the land around it.

The keep is a tower with a wall around it.

The walls of the tower are very high.

You get to the keep by a bridge.

Source A

An early Norman castle drawn in 1994. It has a **keep** (a tower defended by a wall), a **motte** (a big mound of earth) and a **bailey** (the area with buildings in front of the castle) defended by a wall.

A battle from the Bayeux Tapestry. ▶ You can see a castle and its motte in the picture.

Source C

Source D

Some early Norman castles were made of wood. Some modern historians have been trying to find out more about wooden castles.

It is difficult to find out about wooden castles. They have rotted away. Sometimes the rotten wood leaves marks in the earth. Then you can see where they have been.

Questions

1 Look at page 78.
List four ways in which we can tell what an early Norman castle looked like.

2 Look at Source C.

  a Find the motte.
  b Find the keep (castle).
  c Find the steps leading to the motte.

3 Look at Source A. Write down 3 things that are different from Source C.

Christians belonged to one Church

All Christians believed in Jesus Christ. They belonged to one Church. The Church was led by the Pope. He lived in Rome.

The Church was powerful

The Church was rich and powerful. It owned a lot of land.

Most churches had wall paintings. They told a story. This painting shows St Michael. He is wearing a red cloak. He is weighing people's souls. He wants to see if they are good enough to go to Heaven. The devil is waiting to take the bad people to Hell.

Death

Life was hard in medieval times. Many adults died. Many children died. They died from plagues and other diseases. Sometimes they died from cold and starvation.

Heaven and Hell

But the Church said there was hope. Good people went to Heaven when they died. It was wonderful in Heaven. But bad people went to Hell.

What was Christendom?

Christendom was the part of the world where Christians lived. This was most of Europe.

Source A

Jerusalem

The most important city for Christians was Jerusalem.

They called it the Holy City. They did not want infidels to own it.

What was an infidel?

An infidel was what Christians called anyone who was not a Christian.

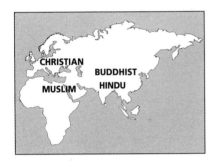

This map shows some of the religions of the world.

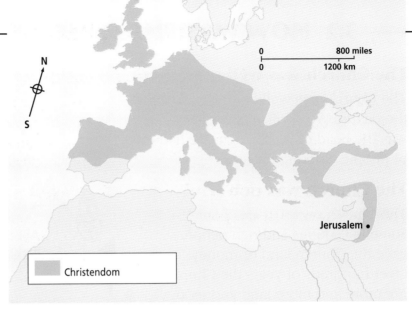

Christendom in about 1200.

Source B

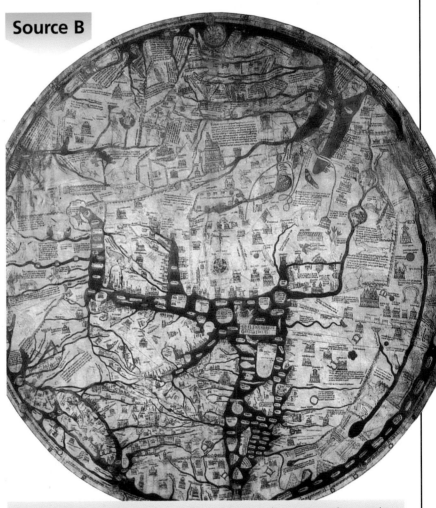

A map of the world drawn in about 1200. It shows Jerusalem at the centre of the world.

Questions

Read **Christians belonged to one Church**.

a What did Christians believe in?

b Who led the Church?

c Where did he live?

The Church was well organised

The Church was well organised. Look at the picture. You will see that the Pope was the head of the Church. He had lots of people working for him.

The Church was rich

The Church owned a lot of land. Sometimes kings and rich people gave the Church land or money. Over hundreds of years the Church got more and more land and money.

Rich people and Heaven

Kings and rich people gave land and money to the Church because they wanted to do good. Then they would go to Heaven when they died.

The Church and ordinary people

The Church had hundreds of priests. They worked in every village. The priests told the people about Christ and the Church. They told them about Heaven and Hell. They made people think about these things.

The Church and schools

The Church ran schools. So many churchmen could read and write, and were well educated. Kings wanted these men to work for them as well as for the Church. This was all right until the kings argued with the Church.

Source A

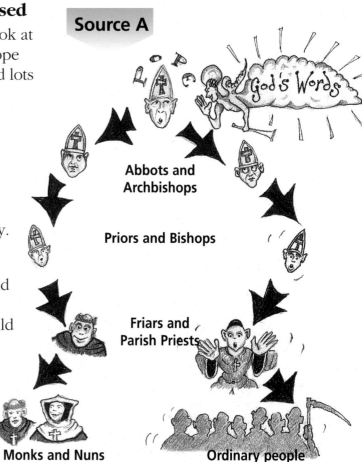

This shows how the Church was organised.

The king was powerful. The Church was powerful. They often argued.

Priests

Most villages had a church and a priest.

Pray for the dead

Read and write (write letters for village people)

Farm his own land

Give food to the poor

Take church services

Collect Church taxes from people in the village

Keep records (write down births, marriages and deaths)

The priest's work.

WILLIAM DE KESTEVENE

William de Kestevene was a parish priest.

The picture below shows what he looked like.

When he was young, he worked for the king. Then he became a priest.

Most priests were poor. But William came from a rich family.

He left money in his will so that a brass picture would be made.

The picture was put up in the church when he died.

Questions

1 Look at Source A.
Who was head of the Church?

2 Read **Priests** and look at the picture.
Write down the jobs the priest did.

Pilgrims and pilgrimages

A pilgrim was a person who travelled to a holy place. The trip was called a **pilgrimage**.

Where did they go?

Some pilgrims travelled to Jerusalem. Some travelled to Rome. Some travelled only to a holy place in Britain. One holy place in Britain was Canterbury.

Why did they go?

Some people were sick. They went to a holy place and asked God to make them better. Other people wanted to thank God for helping them.

Some people went on a pilgrimage as a break from everyday life. They wanted to spend time thinking about God.

The holy places and relics

The holy places might be big churches. Often these churches had a **relic**. A relic was a bit of a saint or holy person. This might be a finger or a lock of hair.

Source A

The Canterbury Tales is a long poem about pilgrims going to Canterbury. It was written by Geoffrey Chaucer. This is one of the pilgrims.

Source B

This badge was worn by pilgrims who visited Canterbury.

Relics

A relic was a part of a saint's dead body, or something that had belonged to a saint. People believed these things were very holy.

Relics were important. If a church had a hand or some teeth from a famous holy person, lots of pilgrims would come to that church.

Holy days

The Church said that some days were holy days. These were days like Christmas and Easter.

Holy days were holidays. People went to church. Then they might celebrate with dancing or singing or seeing a holy play.

Plays and processions

Holy plays were put on in towns. The stage was a painted cart. The big churches put on processions. All the priests dressed in their robes and carried banners. They went all round the town. Then there was a feast and a bonfire.

Source C

Pilgrims gave money or something special to a holy place. Here are a few of the things given to Hereford Cathedral in August 1307:

- **450 gold rings**
- **70 silver rings**
- **108 walking sticks**
- **1,200 wax eyes.**

Thomas Cantilupe was the saint at Hereford. Pilgrims prayed for his help. They left all sorts of gifts at his tomb.

Questions

1 Read **Pilgrims and pilgrimages**.
   What was a pilgrim?

2 Look at Source C.

   a Write down the things that show people were asking for help with walking or giving thanks for walking better.
   b Write down the things that were going to make the cathedral richer.

3 Read **Relics**.

   a What was a relic?
   b Why were relics important?

Source D

Shepherds dancing at Christmas time. Taken from a manuscript made in the 15th century.

York Abbey in 1132

York Abbey was a big monastery. The monks had to live by the strict **Rule of St Benedict** – no speaking, and lots of work and praying.

By 1132 the monks did not live by these rules any more. They had lots of land and money. They lived a comfortable life.

Some monks rebelled

Some monks rebelled. They said they wanted to go back to the Rule of St Benedict. Other monks said no. They liked the comfortable life.

Archbishop Thurstan

Archbishop Thurstan arrived at York Abbey. He found the monks fighting. So he took away the monks who wanted a stricter life. He gave them some land to build a new abbey.

Source B

From the Rule of St Benedict.

- All monks must work in the kitchen.
- All monks must work on the farm or in reading prayers.
- A mattress, a blanket and a pillow is enough bedding.

Source A

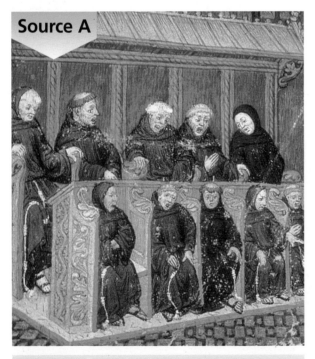

A painting of monks during a church service.

Source C

This is a description of where Fountains Abbey was built.

The land was thick with thorns. It lay between mountains.

Here the monks made shelters to keep off the harsh winter.

They worked to build a small church and to grow food to eat.

Source D

The artist has painted Fountains Abbey as he thinks it looked in the 1400s.

Source E

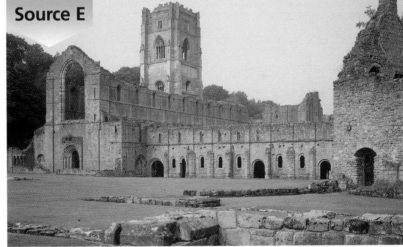

A modern photograph of Fountains Abbey in North Yorkshire.

Questions

1 Read **York Abbey in 1132**.

  a What was York Abbey?
  b What did the monks have to live by?
  c What was the Rule of St Benedict?

2 Read Source B.

  a What sort of work did the monks do? Find three sorts.
  b Write down the three pieces of bedding a monk was allowed.

Many monks

By 1300, one person in every 200 was a monk. The monks lived together in **monasteries**. They did many jobs:

growing vegetables	praying
keeping animals	reading
cutting wood	writing
cooking	cleaning
building	growing herbs for medicine.

Monks' clothes

Monks at Fountains Abbey wore woollen habits or robes. Each monk had:

1 habit (robe)	1 belt
2 cowls (hoods)	1 tunic
2 pairs of slippers	a knife
2 pairs of boots	handkerchiefs
2 pairs of blankets	needles
several pairs of socks	things to write with

Source A

The monks made beautiful books. Sometimes they copied out old books. Sometimes they wrote history books or books about medicine. They painted pictures in the books too.

Historians are not sure how the monks' habits (robes) were made. The monk below has a tunic over his habit.

cowl

habit

tunic   slippers

Source B

A monk painted this picture. It shows the monk in charge of the wine cellar. Some monasteries made wine.

The Rule of St Benedict said that monks must not speak. So they used sign language. Here is one of the signs.

This sign meant a person who had been killed for believing in Jesus Christ.

How the monks lived at Fountains Abbey

At first, the monks were very poor. They built a small church. Then they started a small farm and kept sheep. The years went by and they kept more sheep.

Then they built a big monastery. This was called Fountains Abbey.

Fountains Abbey grows rich

Rich people wanted to show they loved God. They gave money to the Abbey. The monks also made a lot of money from sheep farming.

Soon the monks were rich. They liked a comfortable life. Like the monks at York Abbey, they too began to forget the Rule of St Benedict.

Questions

1 What does Source B show?

2 Look at Source A.

   a What did the monks make?

   b What sort of books did they write?

3 Read **Monks' clothes**.

   a What were the monks' habits made from?

   b What tells you that the monks did their own sewing?

3.6 NUNS AND NUNNERIES

Monks and nuns

A **monk** was a man who wanted to serve God. A **nun** was a woman who wanted to serve God. There were fewer nuns than monks. Most women got married or worked as servants.

Why did women become nuns?

Some women did not want to get married and have children. Nuns learnt to read and write. They also learnt to run a big organisation. Some women liked this better than being wives and mothers.

Nunneries

The places where nuns lived were called **nunneries**. Many nunneries were poor because rich people gave more money to monasteries than to nunneries.

Nunneries changed

At first, nuns were well educated. They knew French, Latin and English.

But by the 1400s this had changed. Bishops said the nuns knew only English. Even worse, the nuns did not work hard for God any more.

Source A

JULIAN OF NORWICH

Julian of Norwich was a holy woman. She lived in a tiny hut by St Julian's Church in Norwich. That is how she got her name.

No one knows her real name.

She was born in about 1342 and lived poorly and simply.

She had many visions and she wrote about them.

One of the things she wrote was:

All will be well and all manner of things will be well.

She trusted in God to make things right.

Look at this painting. In the top row, a nun is pulling the bell rope. This is calling the nuns to church. This nun was also in charge of repairing the church building. The abbess is holding a crook or crosier. She was in charge of all the nuns. Another nun is holding the keys to the wine cellar.

A comfortable life

Over the years, the nunneries became richer – just like the monasteries. The nuns got used to a comfortable life. This was like the monks at Fountains Abbey.

The records of some nunneries show that the nuns spent money on parties at the New Year. They had May Day games and paid actors to put on plays for them at Christmas.

A nun going on a pilgrimage to Canterbury in the 1300s.

Nuns often helped in hospitals, or looked after travellers.

Source C

A modern historian writing about nuns in the 1400s.

Nuns wore golden hairpins and silver belts.

They kept pets. Dogs were the favourite pets, but nuns also kept monkeys, rabbits and birds.

They sometimes took animals to church with them.

Questions

1 Read **Monks and nuns**.
   What was a nun?

2 Look at Source B.
   What jobs did nuns often do?
   Find two jobs.

What the king had to do

Be a good judge in a law court

Lead his army into battle

Ride on horseback all over his kingdom

Keep control of the earls

Man or woman?

Most people thought that a man should be king. They thought women were not strong enough.

When Henry I died, he left only one living child. This was a girl called Matilda.

There was trouble ahead.

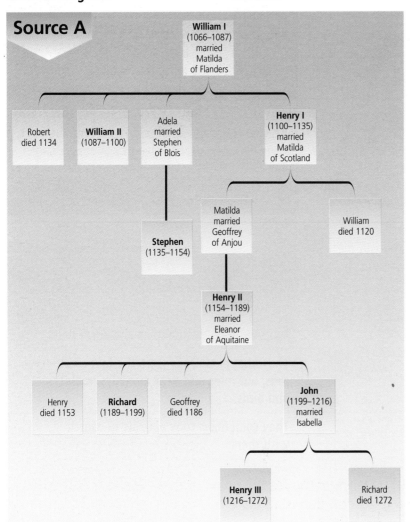

Source A

William I (1066–1087) married Matilda of Flanders

Robert died 1134

William II (1087–1100)

Adela married Stephen of Blois

Henry I (1100–1135) married Matilda of Scotland

Stephen (1135–1154)

Matilda married Geoffrey of Anjou

William died 1120

Henry II (1154–1189) married Eleanor of Aquitaine

Henry died 1153

Richard (1189–1199)

Geoffrey died 1186

John (1199–1216) married Isabella

Henry III (1216–1272)

Richard died 1272

Family tree of English kings.

The dates in brackets are the years they reigned.

Question

Look at **What the king had to do**.

Write down the four things the king had to do.

MATILDA V. STEPHEN

Henry I had two children – William and Matilda.

William drowned in 1120.

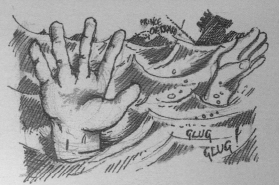

Henry made the earls swear to help Matilda.

Many earls did not want a woman to rule. They made Stephen, the king's nephew, king.

I SWEAR!

Source B

From the Anglo-Saxon Chronicle, 1137. This describes England when Stephen was king.

The earls filled the country full of castles.

They used the castles against the King.

Questions

1 Look at Source B. From reading this, do you think Stephen was a strong king or a weak king?

2 Read **What happened next?** What did Stephen agree with Matilda?

What happened next?

Matilda and Stephen fought for fourteen years. In the end Matilda gave up. But Stephen agreed that Matilda's son would be the next king.

How did Henry get his empire?

Anjou from his father

Normandy from his mother (Matilda)

Henry II

Aquitaine from his wife

England from his cousin (Stephen)

Find the places on the map on page 95.

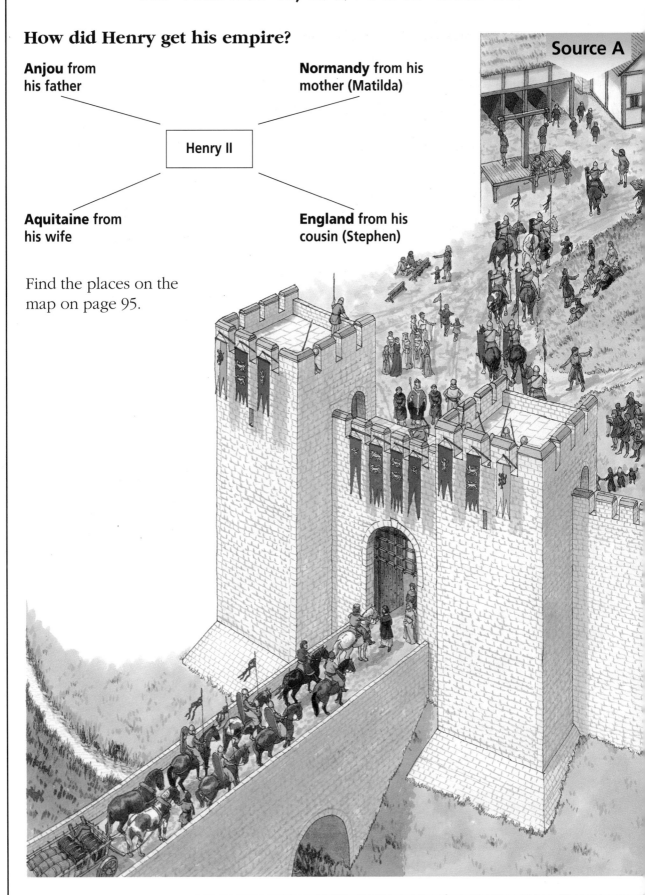

Source A

Putting the problems right

The war between Matilda and Stephen caused lots of problems.

When Henry II became King of England in 1154, he wanted to put these problems right. He wanted to make sure he was a strong king.

This is what Henry did:

- He had all new castles pulled down.

- He sent all foreign soldiers out of England.

- He took back all the land that Stephen had given away.

- He asked the earls for money so that he could pay an army.

- He set up law courts and judges. Sometimes Henry was a judge himself.

Henry II and his followers ride to Orford Castle, in Suffolk.

The King is going to be a judge at one of the courts there.

Henry II's empire.

Source B

From a letter written by Henry's secretary.

Although his legs are sore from hard riding, Henry never sits down.

Often he gets up in the middle of the night and sets off somewhere. Men run about like mad and pack horses are loaded quickly.

Questions

Look at Source A. What is going on in the castle? Choose from the list below:

1 Children playing
2 Men watching TV
3 Men in the stocks
4 Women talking
5 Men being hanged
6 Women hanging out washing
7 Soldiers on guard
8 People cooking
9 People carrying food
10 Soldiers fighting

4.3 CHURCH V. STATE: THE MURDER OF AN ARCHBISHOP IN 1170

Henry II wanted control

When Henry became king, he wanted to control three things:

- He wanted to control the earls.
- He wanted to control the law courts.
- He wanted to control the Church.

The Church and the king

The Church was very strong. It had its own law courts. Henry hated this and thought of a clever plan.

He had a great friend called Thomas Becket. He would make Thomas head of the Church in England. Then he would control the Church.

But Thomas said no. He told Henry that, if he was head of the Church, then the Church would come first.

Source A

This picture of the murder of Thomas Becket was painted in about 1200.

Thomas Becket becomes Archbishop of Canterbury

The king did not listen to what Thomas said. He made Thomas do as he was told.

In 1162 Thomas became Archbishop of Canterbury (the head of the Church of England). It was a disaster.

The quarrel, 1164–70

Henry made a law saying that the king's law courts were more important than the Church law courts. But Thomas did not agree to this. So Henry sent Thomas to live in France.

They did not speak to each other for six years.

Thomas comes back

Thomas came back to Canterbury in 1170. But as soon as Thomas came back, he and Henry quarrelled again.

Henry lost his temper

This time Henry really lost his temper. Four knights heard him shouting. They wanted to please the king, so they decided to murder Thomas Becket.

Source B

An eyewitness describes the murder of Thomas Becket.

On 29 December 1170, the four knights rode into Canterbury. They found Thomas and told him to leave the country. Thomas refused. There were some monks with him. They rushed Thomas into the cathedral. They thought he would be safe there. But the knights followed. They struck Thomas down in front of the altar. They sliced through his skull and his blood and brains splattered over the floor of the cathedral.

Questions

1 Read **Henry II wanted control**.
Write down the three things Henry wanted to control.

2 Read **The quarrel, 1164–70**.

  a What did Henry make a law saying?
  b Did Thomas agree with Henry's law?

3 Read Source B.
What happened to Thomas?

What happened?

- People collected Becket's blood. They believed it would make miracles happen.

- The Pope made Thomas Becket a saint.

- Ever since 1170 pilgrims have gone to Canterbury to pray at Becket's tomb.

- The Church kept its own law courts.

- The King kept on saying who should be archbishop.

King John

Henry II's younger son, John, became king in 1199. He did not keep control. Under King John, the barons were very strong. Barons were noblemen who paid for the king's army through their taxes.

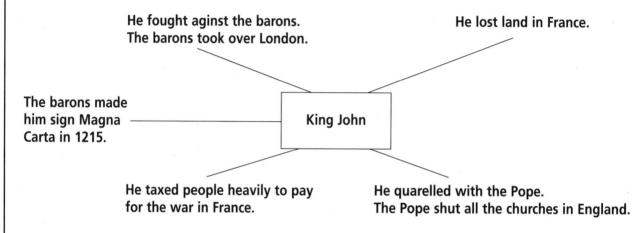

He fought aginst the barons. The barons took over London.

He lost land in France.

The barons made him sign Magna Carta in 1215.

King John

He taxed people heavily to pay for the war in France.

He quarelled with the Pope. The Pope shut all the churches in England.

This picture of King John signing Magna Carta was painted in the 1800s.

Source A

King John signs Magna Carta

The barons were angry with King John. They said that his taxes and laws were unfair. The barons met King John near Windsor Castle and made him sign Magna Carta. 'Magna Carta' means 'Great Charter', and it said that John must rule well.

What did the Magna Carta say?

Magna Carta was really for the barons. It did not help ordinary people much. Here are some of the things it said.

- The barons will give money for the king's army only if they want to.

- No man can be put on trial unless there are good witnesses.

- No free man can be sent to prison except by the law of the land.

- All merchants can travel safely in England.

- If you have done something wrong, you cannot pay to get out of prison.

Questions

1 Read **King John**.

   a When did John become king?
   b Who were the barons?

2 Read **What did the Magna Carta say?** Write down the one you think is most important for ordinary people.

Later King John said he had been forced to sign Magna Carta. So he said that it did not count. The barons were angry and started to fight John again.

King John died suddenly in 1216. The new king was nine years old. So the barons got their way.

ELEANOR OF AQUITAINE (1122–1204)

Eleanor was King John's mother. She was very strong willed. Even when she was over 70 years old, she led an army for her son, John.

These are the sort of clothes that Eleanor and other rich women wore.

5.1 WHAT WERE THE CRUSADES?

A crusade or Holy War

A **crusade** was a war against people of a different religion. Christians and Muslims had different religions. They fought to control the Holy Land. The main city of the Holy Land was Jerusalem.

The First Crusade

The Muslims took over Jerusalem in 1087. The Pope was head of the Christian Church. He asked all Christians to go and take Jerusalem back.

Thousands of Christians walked, rode and set sail for Jerusalem. They were called **crusaders**.

Other crusades

There were more crusades.

They dragged on for well over 200 years.

Muslims   Jerusalem   Christians

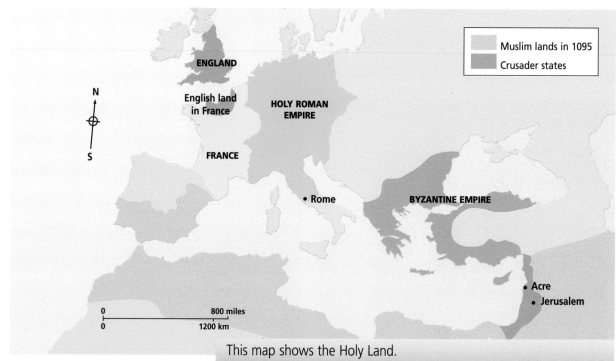

This map shows the Holy Land.
The areas coloured dark orange were places that Christians tried to control.

Some reasons for going on a crusade.

What Saladin said

Saladin was a great Muslim leader. He did not understand why the Christians kept coming to the Holy Land to fight. He said:

- It was a long way to come.
- There were more Muslims than Christians.
- The Christians always gave up in the end and went home.

Questions

1 Read **A crusade or Holy War**.

   a What was a crusade?

   b What was the main city of the Holy Land?

2 Look at the picture above. Write down the main reasons why people went on crusades.

The city of Acre

The city of Acre is in the Holy Land. In 1189, during the Third Crusade, the Christians laid siege to the city. The siege went on for two years.

What was the siege like?

The Christians sat outside the city. The Muslims sat inside. Neither side gave up. The siege went on day after day. It went on month after month.

The Muslims were starving inside the city. But the Christians were starving too.

It was very hot. There was nothing to eat. The soldiers killed and ate their own horses. Sometimes they did not even skin them. They chewed bones left by dogs. They flung themselves on the ground and ate plants.

King Richard I arrives

In 1191 King Richard arrived with more soldiers. He stopped every bit of food getting to Acre.

A month later the Muslims gave up.

This picture of the siege of Acre was painted in 1280.

The soldiers are wearing armour. But many soldiers threw their armour away. It was too hot and too heavy to wear.

KING RICHARD I (1189–99)

Richard was King of England and a Christian soldier. He was brave and loved going on crusades. But he often argued with other kings and with his family.

A Muslim soldier.

A Christian soldier.

Source A

102

This picture, painted in about 1280, shows women attacking their enemies.

Women crusaders

The King said women must not go on crusades. But some women did. They went to fight, or to look after the soldiers.

Some of them were wives. Some women joined the crusade when it got to the Holy Land.

Washerwomen

Women who washed clothes for a living were allowed to go on crusades. So there were washerwomen at the siege of Acre.

Acre was near the sea. So they probably did the washing in sea water.

Catching the washerwomen

The washerwomen were very fierce. If the Muslims caught any washerwomen by mistake, they sent them straight back to the crusaders.

ONE WOMAN

Some women were carrying earth to fill the ditch round the city. One woman was cut down by a Muslim spear. Her husband ran to her. She asked him to use her dead body to fill the ditch.

Question

Read the box **Richard I (1189-99)**.
Write down one sentence about Richard.

Things people brought back from the crusades

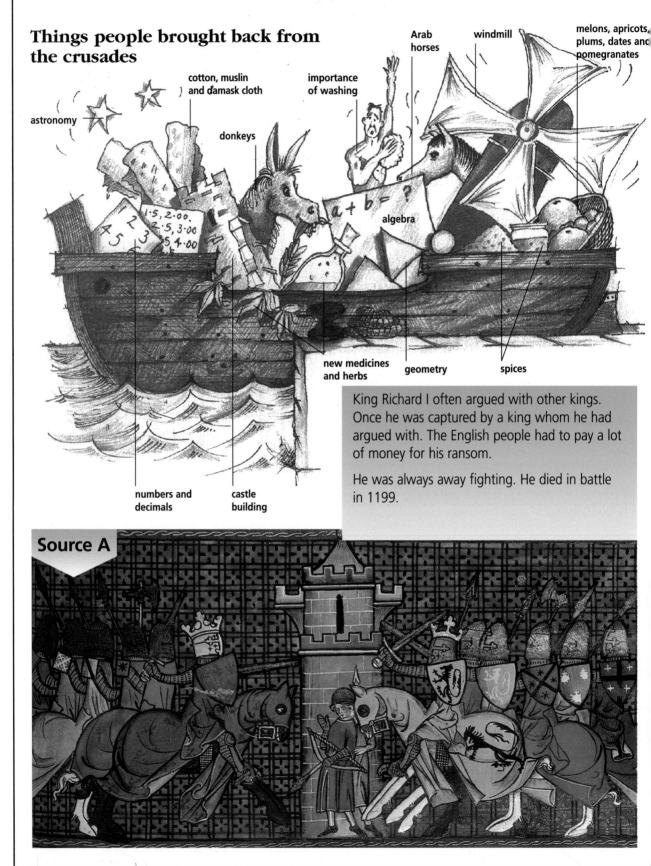

astronomy

cotton, muslin and damask cloth

donkeys

importance of washing

Arab horses

windmill

melons, apricots, plums, dates and pomegranates

algebra

numbers and decimals

castle building

new medicines and herbs

geometry

spices

King Richard I often argued with other kings. Once he was captured by a king whom he had argued with. The English people had to pay a lot of money for his ransom.

He was always away fighting. He died in battle in 1199.

Source A

Learning from the Muslims

The crusaders did not fight with the Muslims all the time. When they were not fighting, the crusaders learnt a lot from the Muslims.

They learnt better ways of building. They learnt the importance of fresh food and regular baths. They learnt how to use Arabic numbers (the numbers we use today).

They also learnt lots of important things about medicine. A Muslim doctor described a visit to a Christian camp in about 1150:

They took me to see a knight with a boil on his leg. I put a **poultice** *on the leg, and it began to heal.*

Then a French doctor came. He sent for a man with an axe. He said to the man 'strike hard and cleanly'. The marrow spurted out of the bone when it was cut. The knight died at once.

How did the Third Crusade affect England?

- Many people died.

- The King was always away fighting.

- The King taxed ordinary people to pay for the crusade.

- The King left his brother John to run the country.

Source B

Muslim doctors were more respected by their patients than European doctors were.

They knew more about drugs and keeping clean.

Question

Look at **Things people brought back from the crusades**.
Write down six of them.

Who owned the village?

The king

I own all the land in England.

I let my Norman lords farm the land.

In return they must fight for me and bring soldiers when I need them.

The lord and the villagers

The lord was given the village land by the king. The villagers worked on the lord's land. They could keep some of the crops they grew.

If there was a war, the villagers had to go with their lord. They had to fight for the king.

The lord

The lord was the most important person in the village.

Lord and lady of the manor, 1250.

The miller was important. The villagers paid him to grind their wheat and barley into flour.

Source A

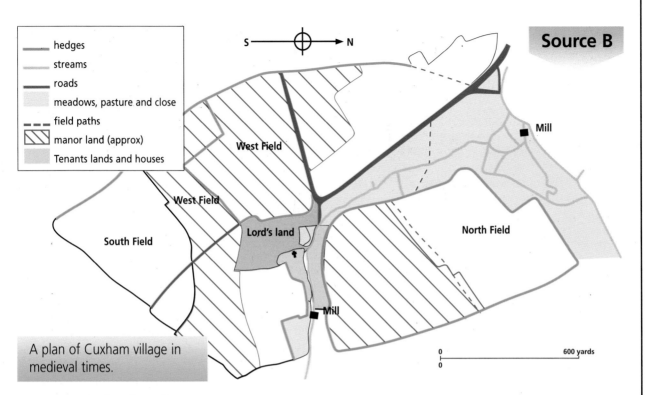

A plan of Cuxham village in medieval times.

Farming the land

There were three big fields. Each year:

- One field grew wheat.
- One field grew barley, oats and rye.
- One field was left to rest.

Each field was divided into strips.

This is a typical field divided into strips:

| Lord's strip |
| Lord's strip |
| Lord's strip |
| Lord's strip |
| Villager A's strip |
| Villager B's strip |
| Priest's strip |
| Villager C's strip |
| Villager D's strip |
| Priest's strip |
| Villager E's strip |
| Villager F's strip |
| Villager E's strip |

ALL GROWING WHEAT

The priest

The priest ran the church in the village.

He baptised, married and buried the villagers.

Questions

Read the boxes **The lord** and **The priest**.

a Who was the most important person in the village?

b What did the priest do?

Cuxham is a village in Oxfordshire.

In medieval times, the lord and the priest were the most important people in the village. But what were the other villagers like?

ROBERT OLDMAN – THE REEVE

Robert Oldman was the **reeve** at Cuxham. One of his jobs was buying and selling crops and animals for the lord.

Robert brewed most of the beer in the village.

In 1313 he went to a place called Abingdon. He bought an ox there and set off home. But he stayed the night at an inn. The ox got away and in the morning it was nowhere to be seen. It took Robert two days to find the ox.

Robert must have been good at his job. He worked as reeve from 1311 until his death in 1349.

The reeve's job

- He made sure everyone did their jobs.
- At harvest time he used extra people to work in the fields.
- He sold spare crops and animals.

Questions

1 Read **The reeve's job**. Write down the 3 things the reeve did.

2 Read **Joan Overchurch**. Write down the two ways that the lord helped Joan when her house was burned down.

Source A

Most village women kept hens.

The village shepherd looked after the sheep.

JOAN OVERCHURCH

Joan Overchurch was married to John. They were comfortably off. They paid rent to the lord instead of working.

But John died in 1311. Soon after, Joan's house burnt down. The lord said she did not have to pay rent for her land for a year.

The lord also gave her some wheat and barley to help her.

Joan passed all her land over to her son Elias. She moved into a small cottage.

JOHN GREEN

John Green was well off. He rented land in Cuxham and other villages too. In 1315 he owned an ox. The only other people who owned an ox in the village were the lord and the priest.

John and his wife, Matilda, had three sons. They were called John, Thomas and Hugh.

Harvest time was one of the busiest times of the year. The whole village was out in the fields working. These pictures of harvest time were drawn in the 1300s.

In the picture below, the workers are cutting wheat and making it into bundles.

In the picture on page 108 a horse and cart is taking the bundles away.

The fishpond

This was used to keep fish in for the lord of the manor. Sometimes the fish got so big that they ate ducklings that were on the pond!

Who worked on the lord's land?

Full time:

- 4 ploughmen

- 1 carter

- 1 cowman and 1 helper

- 1 shepherd

- 1 gardener

Part time

- 1 woman to change barley into malt (for beer)

- 1 pig keeper

- 1 blacksmith

- Extra men and women at harvest time

- Builders and thatchers (roof makers)

The barns

The barns were used to store:

wheat barley hay straw oats peas and beans.

The lord's house

This house was made of stone.

The living rooms were on the first floor.

The lavatory was built over the stream.

What happened to the crops?

Wheat
- Some sold, some for seed, some for wages, some for the lord

Barley and oats
- Some sold, some barley for beer, some oats to feed animals

Apples
- Sold as fruit or cider

Vegetables
- Eaten by lord and servants

Questions

1 Look at the picture.

  a What was the fishpond for?

  b What were the barns for?

2 Read **What happened to the crops?**
  What happened to the wheat?

What did people do all day?

Got up at sunrise.
Worked in the fields.

Midday meal in the fields –
beer, bread and cheese.

Worked all afternoon.

Supper and to bed
at nightfall.

Food

To eat
Bread was eaten all year round. So was cheese and bacon. But some food was difficult to store. Cherries were eaten only in the summer.

To drink
Most families made their own beer. It was more watery than beer is today.

Special jobs

Some people had special jobs. They worked as shepherds, pig keepers, cowmen, thatchers, blacksmiths or carpenters.

Some villagers at work. They are weeding thistles from a field, carding wool (brushing the wool to straighten it) and spinning the wool.

Source A

Time off

The villagers worked from sunrise to sunset. But they had Sunday off.

Sundays and holy days

On Sundays and holy days, the villagers had to go to church. But they did have some time to themselves. Most villagers had about 15 holy days a year. This is where the word 'holiday' comes from.

Easter

One of the great holy days was Easter. The Church celebrated Jesus Christ. Everybody celebrated the spring. Winter was hard and there was not much food. Now, at Easter, the hens started laying eggs again. The cows were giving milk. There was a feast for everyone.

Babies and children

Babies were wrapped tightly in cloth strips. This made them sleep a lot.

Their mothers took them to work. They hung them on a hook or a branch.

Children had jobs. They picked stones off the fields or they scared birds from the seed.

As they got older, they were given harder jobs.

Jobs in the year

Spring:
- Plough.
- Sow seed.
- Shear sheep.
- Put animals outdoors.

Summer:
- Harvest.
- Pick fruit.

Autumn:
- Thresh.
- Plough.
- Sow winter wheat.
- Store hay.
- Kill pigs.
- Put meat in salt.

Winter:
- Mend tools.
- Mend fences.
- Put animals in barns.

All year:
- Work in garden.
- Brew beer, make cheese, spin wool.

Questions

1 Look at the box **Food**.

   a Write down the 2 sorts of fruit shown.

   b Write down any other fruit you eat. Do you know what country each comes from?

2 Read **Jobs in the year**. What time do you think was the busiest?

England and Ireland

England wanted to control Ireland. But Ireland was hard to control.

- It was separated from England by sea.
- It was big and split into lots of kingdoms.

Irish kings fighting

The Irish kings fought each other. One of the kings was **Dermot McMurrough**. He was king of a place in Ireland called Leinster.

But after he lost a big battle in 1152, Dermot McMurrough fled to England.

Henry II and Dermot

King Henry II of England said he would help Dermot. There were two sides to this:

1 Dermot swore **fealty** to Henry.
This meant Dermot would be loyal to Henry.

2 Henry said he would help Dermot against the other Irish kings.

Henry II
English king

Dermot
King of Leinster

Other Irish kings

Henry saw himself as top king.

The English lords who went to Ireland often became Irish themselves:

Many of them have given up their own language (English). Instead they use the language and the ways of life of the Irish.

Source A

An Irish carving from medieval times. The Irish lords have long hair and beards. The Normans said this made the Irish look wild.

DERMOT AND STRONGBOW

Who was Dermot McMurrough?

He was a big, fierce man. In 1131 he was 20 years old. He had an argument with the Abbess of a nunnery. People said he won the argument. He kidnapped the Abbess, killed all the nuns and burned the Abbey to the ground.

Strongbow was an English lord. He went to Ireland and fought for Dermot McMurrough. They won. Strongbow married Dermot's daughter.

Always fighting

Dermot fought all the other kings and lords. He kidnapped one lord's wife and burned all his castles down. In the end Dermot himself was driven out of Ireland. He fled across the sea and met Henry II.

Back in Ireland

Dermot got back his land with Henry's help. He was as fierce and warlike as ever. Some other Irish kings captured Dermot's son and said they would kill him if Dermot did not stop. Dermot said go ahead and kill him – so they did. Dermot died in 1171.

Death of Dermot

When Dermot died in 1171, Strongbow became King of Leinster.

Source B

A painting from about 1200 of a Norman knight in Ireland. He has English armour, but has grown long hair and a beard, like the Irish.

Henry II and Strongbow

Henry was worried. Strongbow was too powerful. Maybe he would attack England. But Strongbow did not want to fight. In the end, Strongbow and Henry met.

1 Strongbow swore fealty to Henry.

2 Henry said he would help Strongbow against the other Irish kings.

Henry as top king

Henry did not go to Ireland with Dermot. But later he went to Ireland with Strongbow.

Several Irish kings swore to be loyal to Henry. This meant that Henry was top king.

Question

Read **England and Ireland**.
Why was Ireland hard to control?
Give two reasons.

William and Wales in 1066

William of Normandy was busy ruling England. So he gave land in Wales to his Norman friends. They gradually took over a lot of South Wales.

Edward I and Wales in 1272

Edward I was a strong king. He wanted to rule all of Wales.

South Wales was easy to control because it was flat and easy to fight in. But North Wales was full of mountains.

Llewelyn and North Wales

Part of North Wales was ruled by **Llewelyn ap Gryffyd**. When Edward I attacked in 1277, Llewelyn led his people into the mountains.

At first, the English could not get at them. But in the end the Welsh had to give themselves up to the English.

Llewelyn and his brother were killed. Edward I had won.

Source A

The Chronicle of Lanercost was written at the time. It describes the punishment of Llewelyn's brother, David:

David had his insides cut out of his stomach for being a traitor. He was then hung for being a thief. His arms and legs were cut off for being a rebel.

Source B

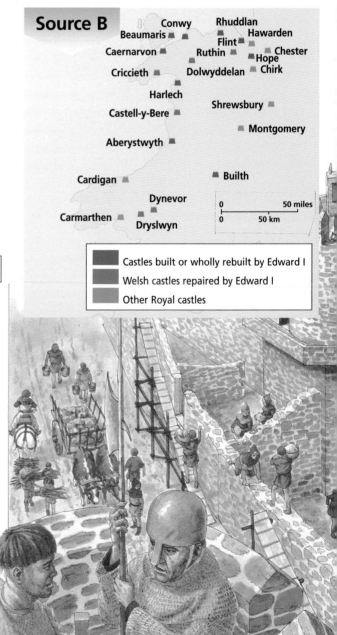

Castles built or wholly rebuilt by Edward I
Welsh castles repaired by Edward I
Other Royal castles

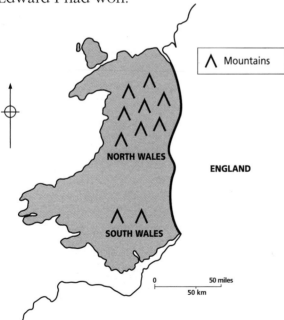

The English took over South Wales. But it was difficult to take North Wales. There were so many mountains.

What did Edward I do to keep the Welsh down?

- Edward built eight new castles.
- He built Conwy Castle in the most important town.
- He built a new town around the castle.
- He made his own son Prince of Wales.

Conwy Castle

Conwy Castle was started in 1283. It took four years to build.

The castle cost £20,000 to build (£2 million in today's money).

On the right you can see a plan of the town of Conwy. The castle is in the bottom right-hand corner.

Men came from all over Britain to build the castle. They worked from the beginning of February to the end of October. They worked from sunrise to sunset. They worked six days a week. It was a magnificent castle. Edward built it to make sure that the Welsh knew the English were staying.

Well designed

The castle was so well built it took only 30 men to defend it and look after it.

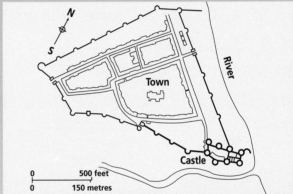

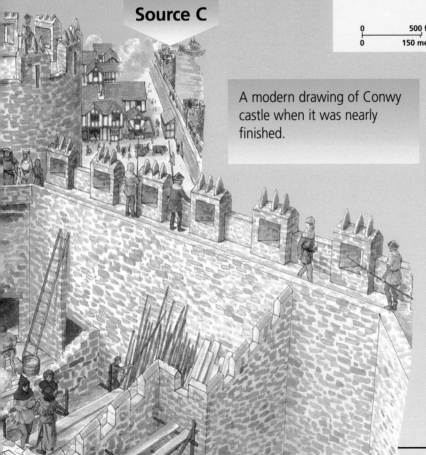

Source C

A modern drawing of Conwy castle when it was nearly finished.

Questions

1 Read **What did Edward I do to keep the Welsh down?** How many castles did Edward build?

2 Read **Conwy Castle**.

   a How much did Conwy Castle cost to build?
   b How much is that worth today?

3 Read **Well designed**. How many men looked after or defended Conwy Castle?

William and Scotland

William of Normandy was busy ruling England. But some of his Norman friends went to live in Scotland.

The years went by. The Normans married into Scottish families and became Scots. They did not want to be ruled by the King of England.

Edward I

Edward I did not like this. He wanted to rule all of England, Wales and Scotland. He had conquered Wales. Now he wanted Scotland.

Edward conquers Scotland

Edward marched to Scotland. By 1305 he had defeated the Scots. He killed their leader, **William Wallace**.

Had Edward won?

Edward had won. But would it last?

Swearing fealty

Edward I forced the Scottish king to swear fealty (loyalty) to him. He seized the Scottish Crown Jewels and the Stone of Scone too. The Stone of Scone is the seat on which Scottish kings were crowned.

Source A

Edward I wanted the Scottish kings to swear fealty to him. But this is what one Scottish king said:

No one has the right to ask me to swear fealty for my kingdom. To God alone will I do this.

Source B

King David II of Scotland with King Edward III of England. They are shaking hands as equals. Compare this to Source A on page 116.

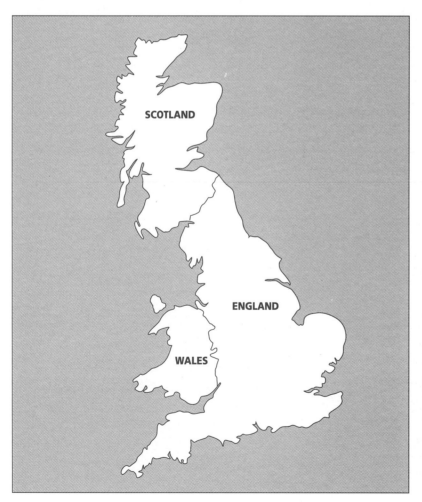

ROBERT BRUCE

Robert Bruce was crowned King of Scotland in 1306. Edward I was furious.

Edward marched to Scotland and killed Bruce's family or put them in prison. But Bruce got away.

Bruce in hiding

Bruce had a few friends. They hid all through the long, cold winter. Sometimes they lived in caves.

The story of Bruce and the spider

Bruce nearly gave up. But one day he saw a spider. It tried over and over again to make its web. Finally it made the web.

This made Bruce think he must go on trying.

Victory at last

Edward I died in 1307. This was Bruce's lucky break. Edward II was a weak king.

Bruce beat the English at the Battle of Bannockburn in 1314. Some years later, Edward III agreed that Scotland should have its own king.

Source C

Robert Bruce, painted in 1306

Questions

1 Read **Edward I**.
What did Edward want?

2 Read **Edward conquers Scotland**.
By what date had Edward defeated the Scots?

3 Read **Robert Bruce**.

   a When did Robert Bruce beat the English?
   b What was the name of the battle?

The population of Britain was growing

The population of Britain was growing in medieval times. More and more people lived in villages and towns. More people needed more food.

Why did towns get bigger?

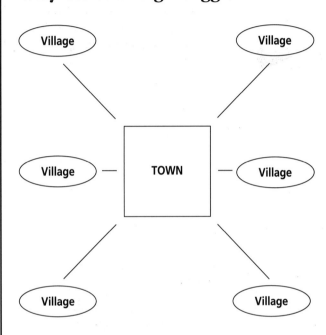

- Villagers grew more food.
- They sold it in the town.
- More people went to live in the town.
- They sold things to the villagers to take home.

London in 1066

London was the biggest town in England. It was a jumble of houses, people, shops and animals.

It was very dirty. People threw rubbish into the streets. They threw rubbish into the rivers. But people also got their water from the rivers and springs.

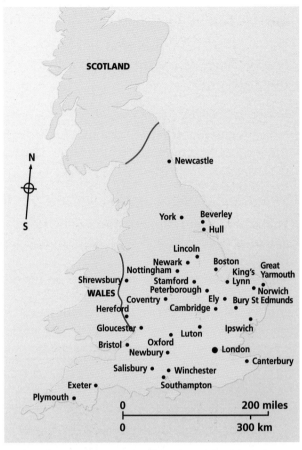

The main towns in England in the 1400s.

London in 1200

London got much bigger. By 1200 the River Thames was filthy. So were the springs and wells nearby. Most people drank beer because it was safer.

Clean water for London

From 1237 people built pipes. These pipes carried clean water from the country. The pipes were made from hollowed-out trees or lead.

This drawing of London Bridge was made around 1500.
The houses were crowded.
The lavatories emptied into the River Thames.

Source B

Part of a letter written in 1349 from King Edward III to the Lord Mayor of London.

This is an order to take away the filth in the streets.

The king has learnt that the city is foul with filth. The air is infected, so people are in danger.

Rich men's houses were made of brick or stone.

Some houses were thatched. Rats and fleas lived in the thatch.

London houses in medieval times.

Poor men's houses were made of mud, sticks and horse-hair.

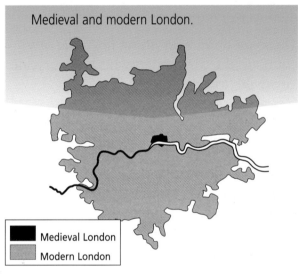

Medieval and modern London.

Medieval London
Modern London

Questions

1 Look at the drawing of London street houses. What lived in the thatch?

2 Look at Source B.

   a Where did the filth go?
   b Why does the King think people are in danger?

Town charters

Many towns grew. They wanted to make their own rules. Below is a list of the sort of things towns needed to have rules about:

- when to shut the town gates
- running markets
- collecting tax money
- having law courts
- street cleaning
- building houses.

But towns needed a **charter** from the king before they could make their own rules.

The town charter of Lincoln

The king gave Lincoln a charter in 1129. Then the people of Lincoln chose a **mayor** and other men to run the town.

These men ran everything from the law courts to the town crier, who let everyone know the town news.

What made Lincoln a rich town?

English wool was the best in Europe. Some of the best wool came from around Lincoln. So there was lots of work for people in Lincoln. The best wool went across the sea to Flanders. They wove very fine wool cloth.

English cloth

The English made rougher, thicker wool cloth. The cloth was used to make clothes for soldiers and working people.

Source A

There were eleven markets in Lincoln. Everyone who sold things at the market had to pay taxes.

On every horse	1d
On every cow	½d
On 24 young sheep	1d
On a big bag of corn	2d

Source B

This picture of a woman weaving cloth was drawn sometime between 1350 and 1375.

Guilds – workers get together

A **guild** was a group of people who worked in the same trade. Here are some guilds:

- shoemakers
- goldsmiths
- butchers
- cloth makers.

In Lincoln there were eleven guilds.

Learning a trade

Apprentice

learns from **master**
for several years

↓

becomes a

Journeyman

↓

then later becomes a

Master

and then teaches
apprentices.

Source C

The people who ran Lincoln decided the prices of things sold at the market. Here are some prices from 1361:

10 eggs	**1d**
3 roast thrushes	**2d**
1 roast pig	**8d**

Source D

This painting, made in 1482, shows a guild master judging the work of men who want to become masters. He will decide whether or not they are good enough.

Questions

1 Read **Town charters**.

   a Write down two things that a town needed to have rules about.

   b Who gave a charter to the town?

   c Which rule would not work in a town today?

2 Read **Guilds – workers get together**. What was a guild?

What is a merchant?

A **merchant** buys from one person and sells to another.

Merchants had ships to bring rolls of cloth to England. They brought spices and furs too. Most merchants were men. But sometimes a merchant died and his wife ran his business.

Abingdon	Soap Clay Iron	Reading	Tin
Alton	Wine Dye Clay Resin Salt	Romsey	Wine Fish Garlic Silk Coal Iron Dye
Andover	Onions Soap Wax Iron Fish		
Bristol	Dye Soap Wine	Salisbury	Wine Fish Dye Flax Soap Canvas Dried fruits Timber Building materials Household furnishings
Exeter	Dye		
Gloucester	Dye Soap Oil		
Honiton	Dye	Wilton	Dye Oil Wine Flax
Leicester	Dye	Winchester	Fish Wine Oil Salt Garlic Iron Soap Dye
Oxford	Wine Dye Millstones		

Source A

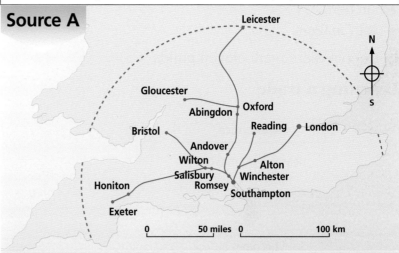

This map shows the goods that were brought into Southampton, and where they came from.

Source B

A picture of a medieval street with shops, painted in about 1460.

A packhorse train.

DAME CLARAMUNDA – A MEDIEVAL BUSINESSWOMAN

Dame Claramunda was married twice. When her husbands died, she ran their businesses.

She was such a good merchant that Henry III asked her to buy all his wine in France in 1258.

This is the way she might have dressed.

Southampton and trade

Southampton was a port. So merchants had ships. They sailed to Europe and brought back wine and silk. They loaded the wine and silk on **packhorses**. Then they sold them all over England.

Source C

This map shows trade between Britain and Europe in the 1450s.

Map labels:

- Bergen — Timber, Fish
- Oslo
- (Timber, Rope, Pitch, Tar)
- Dublin — Cattle, Hides
- Hull
- Boston
- Lübeck
- Danzig — Corn, Timber, Furs
- Wool, Cloth, Tin
- London
- Hamburg
- Bristol
- Southampton
- Antwerp
- Ghent — Cloth, Dyestuffs, Household goods
- Bruges
- Rouen
- St Malo — Linen, Canvas
- Nantes
- Salt
- Alum, Sweet Wines, Silk, Spices, Glass, Luxury goods
- Venice
- Bordeaux — Wine, Woad
- Genoa
- Bilbao
- Florence
- Lisbon — Wine, Oil, Iron, Leather, Wax, Fruit
- Seville
- Málaga

0   800 km

Questions

1 What does a merchant do?

2 Look at Source A.

  a What did merchants buy in Bristol?

  b What did they buy in Winchester?

  c What did they buy in Reading?

  d What did they buy in Exeter?

3 Read **Dame Claramunda.**

  a What did Dame Claramunda do when her husbands died?

  b Why did Henry III ask her to buy his wine?

Bells not clocks

When the sun came up, the bell ringer rang the town bell. The town gates were opened up. At night the bell ringer rang the bell. The gates were closed.

Baths and lavatories

People went to public bath-houses. They used outside lavatories, or poured their waste into the street.

You can see the channel in the street for the waste to run down.

Street cries

Lots of women, men and children sold things on the street. Here are some of the things they sold:

hot apple pies   hot mutton pies hot oatcakes   fresh herrings   cherries apples   rabbits.

They shouted out what they were selling.

A well-off person's house in medieval times. This is a modern painting.

Getting ill

Doctors charged a lot of money. So the women who looked after their families often made their own medicine:

feverfew for fevers and headaches

sage tea for a sore throat

nettle tea for aching bones.

Source A

Cooking

Some houses did not have a kitchen. So women took uncooked bread to a baker. He cooked it in his oven.

Sometimes women or servants took food such as fruit to a pie-maker so he could make the pastry and cook the pie.

Question

Look at the picture.
Find the following:

The fire

The water stored in the house

The windows

The cradle

The broom

The man carrying water

The woman pouring waste onto the street.

The channel carrying rubbish and waste away.

Kitchens

Kitchens were often built in the yard. This was because the kitchen might catch fire.

Most kitchens had bunches of twigs for whisking eggs and cream. There were pots and pans, knives and things for grinding herbs and spices.

What was the Black Death?

The Black Death started in 1346. It was a terrible disease.

Most people died in a few days. It killed millions of people and animals.

Where did it start?

The Black Death started in the East. Then it spread all over Europe.

Sailors caught the Black Death and then they sailed home. The Black Death came with them.

The Black Death moved quickly through towns. People in towns lived very close together. There were also more rats and other animals in towns to pass on the disease.

How the Black Death spread

The Black Death was carried by fleas which lived on rats. These fleas gave people and animals the Black Death by biting them.

Source A

Burying people who died of the Black Death.

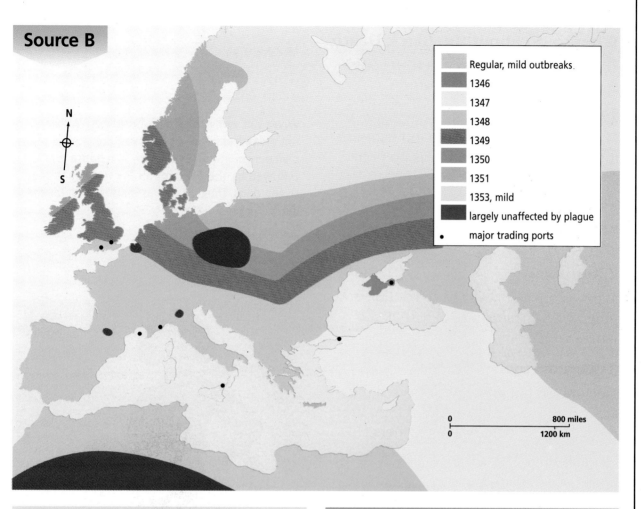

Source B

Regular, mild outbreaks.
1346
1347
1348
1349
1350
1351
1353, mild
largely unaffected by plague
• major trading ports

0 — 800 miles
0 — 1200 km

How the Black Death spread, 1346–53.

Source C

A writer in Italy said that God sent the Black Death to punish people.

God sent the Black Death in the East first. Then it spread through the world.

This terrible sickness was carried by sick people from the East.

By sight, or touch, or breathing on others, they killed everyone.

Signs of the Black Death

- Big swellings in the armpit and groin.
- The swellings turned black.
- Most people died.

Questions

1 Look at the box **How the Black Death spread**.

   a What animals gave people the Black Death?

   b How did these animals give the Black Death to people?

What to do about the Black Death

There were three things a person could do if they had the Black Death.

1 Get ready to die

Many people believed that God had sent the Black Death. So there was no point trying to cure it.

All you could do was say sorry to God for doing bad things. Then you would go to Heaven.

2 Run away

Many people ran away from London and other towns. Sometimes they took the illness with them.

3 See a doctor

Doctors did not know what caused the Black Death. Some took blood from the patient, or gave them herbs. Others charged huge sums of money for cures that did not work.

Trying to control the Black Death

The people who ran some of the towns tried to control the Black Death. They tried to keep sick people away from the others, and to bury dead bodies quickly.

Dying properly

Some people thought that to get to Heaven you had to die properly. This meant seeing a priest before you died and then having a proper burial.

But many people did not have these things. This made their families very upset.

Source A

This is what a writer in Italy said about the Black Death.

Wives ran away from their husbands. Brothers ran away from each other. Even the clothes of a victim could kill. One death in a house was followed by the death of all the rest, right down to the dogs. Doctors did not have a cure for the Black Death.

Source B

The doctor is taking blood from a patient.

Some doctors thought that too much blood made you ill.

Questions

Look at the picture above.

a Write down one idea that people had about what caused the Black Death.

b Why would keeping the streets clear of rubbish help to stop the Black Death?

Many died

The Black Death killed more than half the adults in Cuxham village.

Money

The new villagers did not want to have to work on the lord's land. So the lord and the new villagers made an agreement.

You pay me for your cottage and land.

You pay us for working for you.

New people came

New people came to live in Cuxham. But often they did not stay long.

It was difficult for the lord to find a man to be the reeve and run the village.

Burning the clothes of people who had died of the Black Death.

Source A

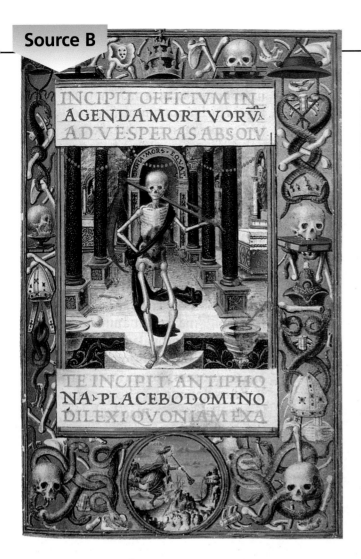

INCIPIT OFFICIVM IN
AGENDA MORTVORV
AD VESPERAS ABSOLV

TE INCIPIT ANTIPHO
NA PLACEBO DOMINO
DILEXI QVONIAM EXA

After the Black Death, pictures of Death appeared all over Europe.

Questions

Read **Robert Oldman and his family**.

a When did Robert die?
b What do you think happened to Richard and Robert?

PEOPLE IN CUXHAM

JOHN GREEN AND HIS FAMILY

John Green and his son John survived the Black Death. But another son, Thomas, died.

After the Black Death, the two Johns mainly kept sheep. One man could look after a lot of sheep. Maybe there were not enough men to plough and dig and grow crops.

ROBERT OLDMAN AND HIS FAMILY

Robert died in March 1349.

Then his wife died.

Then his son John died.

We do not know what happened to the other sons, Richard and and Robert. They are not heard of again in the lord's records.

JOAN OVERCHURCH

Joan was dead before the Black Death. But her son Elias and his family died.

HENRY GARDENER

Henry Gardener survived the Black Death. He even became better off because so many other people died.

9.4 HOW DID THE BLACK DEATH AFFECT OTHER PLACES?

We have seen how the Black Death affected people in Cuxham. But what was it like in other places?

Many parts of France

About one in ten lived.

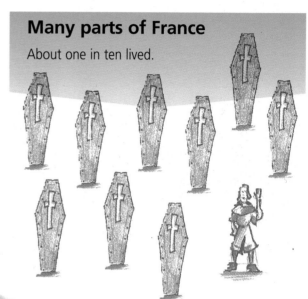

Genoa, Italy

One in seven lived.

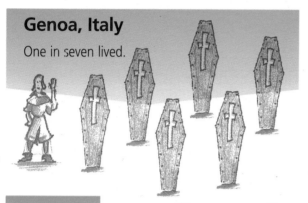

Source A

Lots of people...

Lots of workers need land, so...

the lord...

need food...

Fewer workers...

Fewer people...

asks for a lot of work, not rent...

lots of land...

need less food..

workers ask a lot for their work...

so food prices go down...

pay rent, work less...

and doesn't let his workers move about.

move about more...

will do extra work but only for pay!

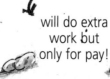

and animals are kept more and need fewer workers.

After the Black Death there were fewer people so workers asked for a lot of money for their work.

England

Only one in ten lived.

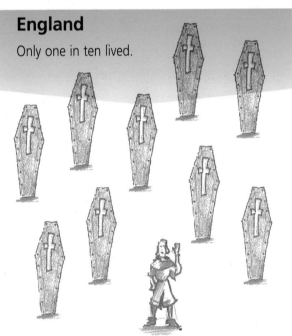

Many monks looked after the sick people with the Black Death. Many of the monks died.

Source C

This is what the King of England said in 1349:

Many farm workers have died. The farm workers who are left want more money. This makes farming difficult.

So we order that any man or woman under the age of 60 must work. They must work for the same money as they got before the Black Death.

Questions

Look at Source A. Read **After the Black Death**. Fill in the gaps in these sentences using the word box opposite.

a After the Black Death, there were _____ workers.

b After the Black Death, the workers asked for _____ money.

c After the Black Death, the price of food went _____.

. a lot of	down	fewer

The Black Death

The Black Death killed thousands of people. Who would plant the crops? Who would look after the chickens, sheep and cows?

Higher wages

The lords who held the land were desperate. There were only a few labourers left. So the lords offered labourers more money.

John Ball

John Ball was a priest. He said that all people were created equal by God. What he said frightened rich people. But poor labourers listened to him and agreed.

The Poll Tax

Poll is another word for head. So the Poll Tax was a tax on heads.

Here is more money. Please work on my land.

4 heads = 4 people to pay Poll Tax.

The king and the lords

The king and the lords did not like the labourers getting more money. So they decided to pass a law in Parliament.

The Statute of Labourers, 1351

This new law was called the Statute of Labourers. It said that labourers must only be paid the same money as before the Black Death.

This made the labourers angry.

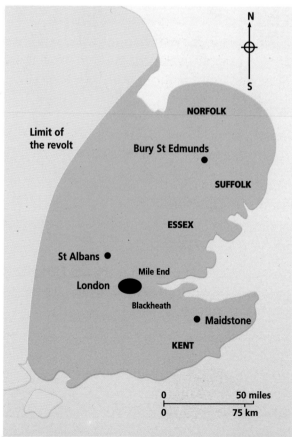

This map shows where the labourers rioted.

Source A

This poem was written at the time of the Peasants' Revolt:

**When Adam dug and Eve span,
who was then a gentleman?**

Source B

John Ball leading a group of peasants. The picture was painted in 1460.

Why did the king set the Poll Tax?

The king needed money to fight France. He taxed everyone over the age of 15 years. This was called the Poll Tax.

What people had to pay

1377   4d per person
1379   4d per person
1381   12d per person

This was a lot of money for a poor person to pay.

What happened?

Labourers in Essex rioted. Labourers in Kent rioted too. They were led by Wat Tyler. They marched on London.

The Peasants' Revolt had begun. Peasant is another word for a poor labourer.

Source C

From the Statute of Labourers.

Men shall work for the same money they were paid before the Black Death or they will be put in prison.

Questions

Read **The Statute of Labourers, 1351**.

a What did the Statute of Labourers say?
b How did the labourers feel about this?

141

Where did the rebels come from?

The peasants who rebelled came from different places. They came from Essex, Kent, Suffolk and Norfolk.

Who were they?

Many of the people who rebelled were poor labourers – but not all.

Peasant rebels in Suffolk

The court records of Suffolk tell us about some of these people.

WILLIAM METEFIELD

William was first in court in 1369. It was said he 'drew blood' from Alice Godhave.

In 1377 he was fined for brewing too much ale.

In 1381 William led a band of peasants in Norfolk. They robbed and looted.

He is never heard of again.

MARGARET WRIGHTE

We know about very few women in the Peasants' Revolt.

Margaret was in court in 1379. She was fined for brewing too much ale.

In 1381 she was accused of killing a judge. But we do not know what happened to her.

JOHN HARAS

We first hear of John when he was on a jury in 1371.

In 1381 he joined a group of peasants attacking a manor.

He was pardoned in 1383.

N

S

● Brandon
● Lakenheath

● Herringswell

■ BURY ST EDMUNDS

SUFFOLK

● Kersey   ● Aldham   ■ IPSW

Fel

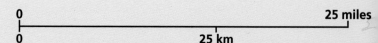

0   25 miles

0   25 km

ADAM ROGGE

In 1360 Adam was in court for arguing with his mother.

In 1361 he was in court for beating up Thomas Elenesfenne.

In 1371 he was in court over money, then later for letting cows get out.

In 1381 Adam was looking after his lord's land. But on 14 June 1381 he joined the peasant rebels.

They attacked houses and stole money.

THOMAS SAMPSON OF KERSEY

Thomas was a rich peasant. In 1381 he owned:
- land in 3 villages
- 72 horses and cows
- part of a ship
- sheep and quite a bit of money.

Collector of the Poll Tax
In 1379 and 1381 Thomas collected the Poll Tax for the king.

Thomas rebels
In June 1381 he changed his mind. He led the peasants against the Poll Tax. In 1383 he was condemned to death. But he was pardoned.

LOWESTOFT ■

JOHN COLE

In 1363 John was fined for refusing to do winter work for his lord.

In 1381 he and others burnt some court records.

In 1384 he was fined for taking part in the Peasants' Revolt. But he argued with the court and did not pay the fine.

In 1385 John was accused of hitting another peasant.

Although he was supposed to be arrested, he is never heard of again.

Questions

1 Read **Where did the rebels come from?**
From which 4 counties did the rebels come?

2 Read the box on **Adam Rogge**.
Why do you think he joined the peasant rebels?

3 Read the box on **Thomas Sampson**.
Why do you think he changed his mind about the Poll Tax?

ve

The peasants march on London

On 12 June 1381, 60,000 peasants from Kent and Essex marched on London. They had hardly any real weapons. But they were determined.

Richard II goes down the river

King Richard II was only 14 years old. He decided to talk to the peasants.

Richard II, Simon Sudbury and Robert Hales set off in the royal barge to go down the river to meet the people.

Simon Sudbury and Robert Hales

These two men were advisers to Richard II. The peasants hated them. The peasants blamed them for the Poll Tax.

As soon as the peasants saw the two men, they shouted out that Sudbury and Hales were the traitors. They must be killed. Quickly the barge turned back.

The peasants are let into London

The people of London supported the peasants. They gave the peasants food. Then the peasants went on the rampage. They burnt the palace of the king's uncle. They burnt the building where legal records were kept.

Richard at the Tower

Richard II was safe in the Tower of London. The peasants rushed there and demanded to see him.

Source A

This painting shows Richard II meeting the peasants in June 1381.

Source B

Part of a speech made by John Ball to the peasants in 1381:

The men we call lords, what makes them our masters?

They live in fine houses. We sweat and work in the fields in wind and rain.

They call us slaves and beat us if we do not serve them.

We have no one to listen to us.

Let's go to the King and explain what it's like. Let's tell him we want it changed.

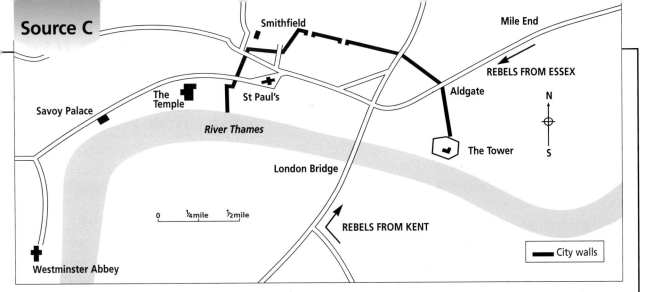

Source C

Smithfield
Mile End
REBELS FROM ESSEX
The Temple
St Paul's
Aldgate
Savoy Palace
River Thames
The Tower
London Bridge
0 ¼mile ½mile
REBELS FROM KENT
Westminster Abbey
N
S
—— City walls

London in 1381 showing the routes the rebels took.

The King meets the peasants

Richard II met the peasants. The leader of the peasants was Wat Tyler. Wat Tyler asked Richard to do four things:

- end serfdom (no one has to stay working for the same lord)
- end labour services (no one has to work so many days a week for the lord for nothing)
- punish the king's advisers
- pardon all the peasants who had rebelled.

Richard agrees to all but one

Richard II would not punish his advisers. So the peasants killed them. They stuck the heads of Simon Sudbury and Robert Hales on poles.

The King meets the peasants again

This time Wat Tyler asked for more. Then no one is sure what happened. There was a scuffle and Wat Tyler fell dying. The peasants raised their bows, ready to fire. But Richard II rode forward. He said:

Would you shoot your king? I will be your leader. Follow me and you will have what you want.

He led them out of London. He persuaded them to go home.

Broken promises

As soon as he could, Richard II broke his promises to the peasants. Many were hanged or fined. Nothing changed.

Source D

Richard II said this to the peasants after the revolt. (A villein was a peasant who had to work for his lord.)

Villeins you were and villeins you shall remain.

Questions

1 Read **The King meets the peasants**.

   a Who was the leader of the peasants?
   b What four things did he ask for?

2 Read **Broken promises**. What happened to many of the peasants?

England and France quarrel about land

After 1066 English kings ruled land in France. The French did not like this. During King John's reign (1199–1216) they took most of the land back. The English did nothing about this until **Edward III** became king.

Why did the Hundred Years' War start?

1 Edward III said he was the rightful King of France.

ENGLAND

V

FRANCE

2 Edward III wanted land in France.

3 Edward III was angry because the French were helping the Scots to raid England.

4 Edward III enjoyed wars and fighting.

The English invade France

In 1337 Edward III invaded France. This started a long war which lasted until 1453. It is known as the Hundred Years' War.

What happened during the Hundred Years' War?

The English won a lot of battles to begin with. But the French fought back. By 1453 the English were left with just the port of Calais. The war cost a lot of money and many people were killed.

A modern picture of the types of people who went off to battle.

Source A

Cannon were used at the Battle of Crécy. Henry V had 75 gunners, who bombarded French towns.

As well as soldiers there were armourers, grooms, priests and doctors. Women joined as helpers.

Some bowmen also used crossbows. These were drawn by winding a handle, and could shoot arrows through armour.

A squire looked after a knight's armour, which packhorses carried. The squire helped the knight to put his armour on.

The Battle of Crécy, 1346

In 1346 Edward III sailed to France again. He had a big army and planned to capture Paris.

The English were chased by the French. They caught up with the English at Crécy. A battle took place.

Edward placed his army at the top of a hill. His men had time to eat and rest. The French had marched a long way and were tired.

The battle was fought on 26 August 1346. Source B tells you what happened.

Source B

Written by a French historian in 1401.

The French had crossbows.

The English had longbows.

It took longer to load a crossbow.

The King of France ordered his crossbowmen to march towards the English. The sun was in their eyes and they were tired.

The English archers fired their arrows. They went so quickly that they fell on the French like a heavy snowstorm. The crossbowmen ran away in panic.

Then English soldiers charged through the French. They had large knives. They killed many barons and knights. The French were beaten.

Questions

1 Look at page 146.
   Which English king started the Hundred Years' War?

2 Read Source B.
   Why did the English win Crécy?

Foot soldiers wore everyday clothes. They carried their own weapons.

English archers had longbows, which they carried wrapped in cloth. They wore leather **jerkins** and carried food in sacks.

A knight wore steel armour, as did his horse. He carried a shield and used an axe or mace to fight hand-to-hand.

Pages served the knights. They were sometimes killed helping knights off their horses during battle.

Henry V sails to France

On 11 August 1415, Henry V sailed to France. He had an army of 6,000 archers and 2,500 knights. Henry wanted to capture land from the French.

Henry V takes Harfleur

In September 1415 the English captured the town of Harfleur. Then came disaster. The Black Death broke out among the English. Many men died.

Henry was worried. He knew his army had been weakened.

The Battle of Agincourt, 25 October 1415

The French were waiting to fight Henry at the village of Agincourt.

Henry ordered his archers to walk towards the French. They got close and then fired a shower of arrows. Many French knights were killed. The English archers fired again and again.

Then the English fought the French with swords. More French soldiers were killed. Others ran from the battlefield. Henry had won a great victory.

Source A

A medieval painting of the Battle of Agincourt.

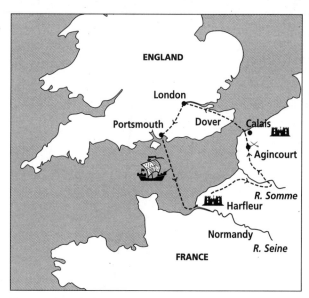

The road to Agincourt.

Battlefield doctors

There were many battles in medieval times. This meant doctors got a lot of practice in treating wounds.

Source B is a 'wound man'. It shows the wounds that doctors said they could heal. It also shows us the weapons used at the time.

Hugh of Lucca

Hugh was a doctor in Italy during the 1200s. He worked with the army in times of war.

He saw many different wounds. This forced him to try out different cures and treatments.

Hugh found out that wine would heal wounds. It helped to keep wounds clean. This was an important discovery.

But some doctors still used the old ointments that did not work.

Theodoric of Lucca

Theodoric was the son of Hugh. He was also an army doctor. He wrote about the ways of healing used by his father (Source C).

Henry V's doctors would have known about these treatments. They may well have used them at Agincourt.

Source B

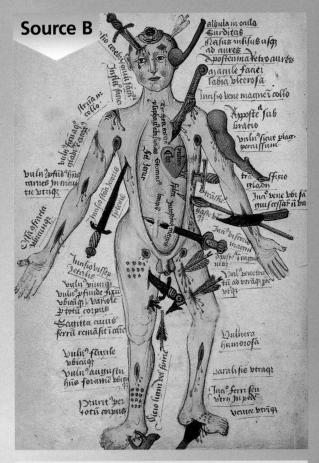

A medieval 'wound man'. It shows the wounds that army doctors could heal.

Source C

This was written by Theodoric of Lucca in 1267.

Every day new methods are being thought of for taking arrows out of a soldier. The army doctors are very clever.

My father used to heal most wounds with just wine. It worked very well. He did not use any ointments.

Questions

1 Look at Source B.
   Write down some of the wounds that doctors said they could cure.

2 Read **Battlefield doctors**.
   Why were army doctors good at treating wounds?

11.3 THE WARS OF THE ROSES: YORK V. LANCASTER

Henry VI of Lancaster

In 1422 Henry VI became the King of England. Henry was from a rich family called the House of Lancaster.

Henry was a weak king, who sometimes had fits of madness.

The House of York was another rich family in England. The York family hated Henry VI and said he was not fit to rule England.

The two families started to quarrel. They both wanted to rule England.

Source B

Ordinary people did not fight in the wars, but sometimes they were attacked by soldiers.

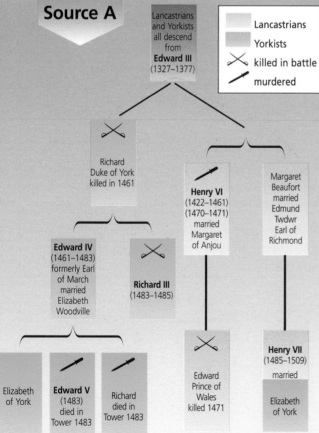

Source A

	Lancastrians
✕	killed in battle
🗡	murdered
	Yorkists

Lancastrians and Yorkists all descend from **Edward III** (1327–1377)

Richard Duke of York killed in 1461

Henry VI (1422–1461) (1470–1471) married Margaret of Anjou

Margaret Beaufort married Edmund Twdwr Earl of Richmond

Edward IV (1461–1483) formerly Earl of March married Elizabeth Woodville

Richard III (1483–1485)

Elizabeth of York

Edward V (1483) died in Tower 1483

Richard died in Tower 1483

Edward Prince of Wales killed 1471

Henry VII (1485–1509) married

Elizabeth of York

The Wars of the Roses

The Lancaster family wore a red rose as their badge. The York family wore a white rose.

The quarrel between the two families turned into a series of battles between 1454 and 1485.

These battles became known as the Wars of the Roses.

Both sides were rich enough to have their own private armies. The ordinary people of England did not fight in the battles. They went on with their lives as normal.

A family tree. It shows the families of York and Lancaster.

The Battle of Towton

Henry VI won the first battles. But in 1461 Henry was beaten by the York family at Towton in Yorkshire.
It was a fierce battle. Thousands were killed.

A river ran through the battlefield. It became blocked with dead bodies and the fields were flooded with blood.

Edward IV of York

After the Battle of Towton, Edward IV of York became king. He was a good soldier and much stronger than Henry VI.

More battles

Henry VI tried to win back the throne, but he was beaten by Edward IV in the battles of Barnet and Tewkesbury.

Murder?

In 1471 Henry VI died in the Tower of London. He was probably murdered on the orders of Edward IV.

Edward IV ruled until his death in 1483.

What would happen now?

The progress of the Wars of the Roses

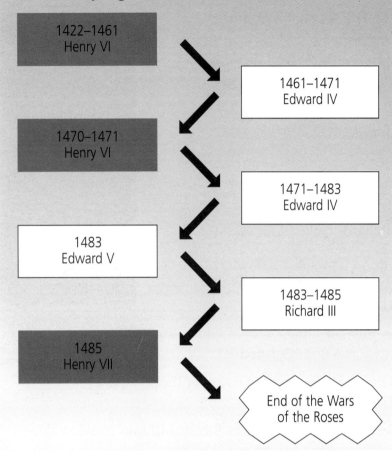

The red boxes show Lancastrian kings, the white boxes show Yorkist kings. The dates shown are the years they reigned.

Questions

1 Read **Henry VI of Lancaster**.
   Why did the York family and the Lancaster family quarrel?

2 Read **The Wars of the Roses**.
   Why were the battles between the two families called the Wars of the Roses?

3 Read **The Wars of the Roses** and look at Source B.
   What happened to ordinary people at this time?

Richard III – a wicked uncle?

Edward IV of York died in 1483. He left two sons:

1 Edward – aged 12.

2 Richard – aged 9.

Both princes were too young to rule England.

This job was given to their uncle – Richard, Duke of Gloucester.

He was a good soldier and was popular with many people.

Source A

Richard III, painted later.

Mystery

In July 1483, the Duke of Gloucester was crowned **Richard III**.

The two princes were living in the Tower of London. They were never seen again.

People began to say that Richard III had murdered them so that he could become the king.

Richard III lost some of his followers. They turned instead to support **Henry Tudor**, of the Lancaster family.

Bones

In 1674 the bones of two young boys were dug up in the Tower.

Some historians say that they are the bones of the princes; others disagree.

What really happened is still a mystery today.

Source B

Written by Sir Thomas More in 1520.

Sir James Tyrell was sent to the Tower with a letter from King Richard.

It said that he should be given all the keys of the Tower for the night.

That night the princes were smothered while they were asleep.

Sir James rode to tell King Richard. He was very pleased.

Henry Tudor

In 1485 Henry Tudor of Lancaster landed in Wales. He had been living in France for his own safety for a number of years.

He was going to win the throne from Richard III.

He marched into England.

People joined his army on the way. He soon had an army of 5,000 men.

The Battle of Bosworth Field 1485

Henry Tudor fought Richard III at Bosworth Field.

Although he had a bigger army, Richard III was beaten. The battle was all over in less than an hour.

Richard was cut down and killed.

There is a story that Richard's crown was found in a thorn bush and given to Henry.

He became Henry VII, the first Tudor king.

The Tudor rose

In 1486 Henry VII married **Elizabeth of York**.

He did this to show that the Wars of the Roses were over.

The white rose of York and the red rose of Lancaster were made into one rose.

The new rose was called the Tudor rose. It was red on the outside and white in the middle.

The Tudor rose. It is a double rose: red on the outside and white in the middle.

Questions

1 Read **Mystery**.
   Why might Richard III have murdered the princes?

2 Read **The Battle of Bosworth Field 1485**.
   What happened at this battle?

3 Read **The Tudor rose**.
   What did Henry VII do to show that the Wars of the Roses were over?

The Roman Empire

(pages 4–65)

amphitheatre large round open stadium used for entertainments.

archaeologists historians who learn about people who lived a long time ago. They study ancient objects dug up out of the earth.

auxiliaries soldiers in the army from the foreign countries Rome had conquered.

barbarians any tribe or people outside the Roman Empire, usually thought to be rough and uncivilised.

biased letting personal beliefs influence what you write or say.

centurion soldier in charge of a group (century) of about 80-100 soldiers belonging to a legion.

centuries a group of soldiers (about 80-100 men) within the cohort.

cohorts a group of soldiers within the **legion**, about 480-600.

consul one of two men who governed Rome and commanded the army.

empire all the countries ruled over by another country.

forum public square or market place in a Roman city used for meetings and business.

hypocaust hot air central heating system used in Roman houses.

legate the commanding officer in control of a **legion**.

legionaries soldiers in the Roman army belonging to a legion.

legions large groups of soldiers (about 5000 men each) in the Roman army.

milecastles regular forts about 1500m apart along Hadrian's Wall protecting England from the Scottish tribes.

mosaics pictures and patterns made out of a jigsaw of coloured stones.

republic the government of a country that is chosen by the people.

sacrifice killing of an animal or person as a gift to please a god or gods.

sources writings and objects that have survived from the past.

standard flag or carving on a tall pole carried by the leading soldier into battle.

strigil a skin-scraper used by bathers after exercise.

tablets flat slabs of stone, wood or wax with writing on.

taxes regular amounts of money demanded from the people by a ruler.

turret small tower built out of a defensive wall and used as a look-out post.

vallum the ditch under Hadrian's wall that probably marked the boundary between England and Scotland.

Medieval Realms

(pages 66–153)

bailey castle wall surrounding the castle courtyard.

charter the written rules about governing the country or a city, agreed between the king and the people and written down.

crusade journey by Christian soldiers to fight the Muslims for control of Jerusalem.

crusaders Christian soldiers who set off to rescue Jerusalem from the Muslims.

Domesday Book this contained all the information collected for William the Conqueror about the size of English villages and farms.

fealty a promise of obedience sworn by the nobles to the king.

feudal system the way people were organised into fighting for the nobles and the king in return for having some land.

guild a 'club' for craftsmen and merchants which looked after them and made sure their work was good. Each craft had its own guild.

infidels people who were not Christians.

jerkin a leather jacket with no sleeves.

keep a high tower inside a castle.

Magna Carta the 'Great Charter' the nobles made King John agree to. It was a list of things that would give the **nobles** more power.

mayor the leader of a town, chosen by the townspeople.

merchants people who bought goods from one person and sold them to another.

monasteries the buildings where **monks** lived and worked.

monk a man who gives up ordinary life to pray and work for God and live in a **monastery**.

motte the mound of earth where a castle is built.

nobles the few most important men in the country next to the king. Usually knights or lords, they were rich and powerful.

Normans the French men who came over to England with William the Conqueror in 1066. They settled in England.

nun a woman who gives up ordinary life to pray and work for God and live in a **nunnery**.

nunneries the buildings where **nuns** lived and worked.

packhorses horses used for carrying luggage.

pilgrimage a journey to a holy place, usually for a special religious reason.

poultice a warm bandage wrapped on a swelling or boil to make it go down.

reeve the person in charge of the farms and the villages belonging to a lord.

relic part of a holy person kept after they have died. The relic was believed to have special powers - even of curing illness.

Rule of St Benedict a set of rules made by St Benedict for **monks** to follow throughout their lives.

Photographic acknowledgements

The authors and publishers would like to thank the following for permission to reproduce photographs:

The Roman Empire (pages 4–65)

Ancient Art & Architecture Collection: 1.1A, 1.1B, 5.1C, 8.1B
Bridgeman Art Library/Tabley House, University of Manchester: 5.1A
British Library: p64, p65
British Library/Bridgeman Art Library: p62
British Museum: 1.2B, p52, 6.5A, 6.6C
University of Cambridge/Aerial photography collection: 7.2B
Colchester Museums: 3.1D
C.M. Dixon: 2.1A, 3.3B, 6.6A
Robert Estall Photo Library: p63
Robert Estall Photo Library/Malcolm Aird: 7.3D
Robert Harding Picture Library: 1.4A
Michael Holford: 4.1A, 4.1B
A K Kersting: 8.1A
Kobal Collection/MGM: 6.2A
The National Trust Photographic Library/ Ian Shaw: 6.4B
Rex Features: 1.4B
Scala/Galleria Borghese, Rome: 6.2C
Scala/Museo della Ciuilta Romana, Rome: 6.1B
Society of Antiquaries of London: 3.2A
Edwin Smith: 5.1E
Werner Forman Archive: 5.1C
York Archaeological Trust: 1.4A

Medieval Realms (pages 66–153)

Aerofilms Ltd: 1.1D
Ancient Art and Architecture: 3.1B
Bibliotheque Nationale, Paris/Bridgeman Art Library: 5.2B, 9.4D, 10.3A
Bibliotheque Royal de Belgium/Bridgeman Art Library: 8.3B
Bibliotheque Royale Albert: 9.1A
Bodleian Library: 2.4A, 3.3B, 3.5A
British Library: 1.1F, 3.4A, 3.5D, 3.6A, 5.3A, 6.1A, 6.2A, 6.4A, 8.1A, 8.2B, 9.2B 6.5A
British Library/Bridgeman Art Library: 3.6B, 4.3A, 8.2D, 10.1B
Masters and Fellows of Corpus Christi College, Cambridge: 1.1E
English Heritage: 2.2A, 3.4D
Giraudon/Bridgeman Art Library: 1.1A
Michael Holford: 2.1A, 2.2B, 2.3A

House of Commons/Bridgeman Art Library: 4.4A
A K Kersting: 3.1A
Lambeth Palace Library/Bridgeman Art Library: 11.2A
Museum of London: 3.3B
National Museum of Ireland: 7.2A
National Portrait Gallery: 11.4A
The National Trust Photographic Library: 3.4E
Scottish National Portrait Gallery: 7.4C
St Mary's Church, North Mimms: 3.2
Trinity College, Dublin: 7.2B
Wellcome Institute Library: 11.2B

Written source acknowledgements

The authors and publishers gratefully acknowledge the following publications from which written sources in the book are drawn. In some sources the wording or sentence structure has been simplified.

The Roman Empire (pages 4–65)

D Birt, *Viking Life*, Longman: p63
A Bowman, *Life and Letters on the Roman Frontier*, British Museum Press, 1994: 3.3C, 7.5F
Julius Caesar, *The Conquest of Gaul*, trans. S A Handford, Penguin, 1982: 7.1B
F R Conwell, *Everyday Life in Ancient Rome*, B T Batsford, 1963: 6.4D
Cassius Dio, *Roman History*, trans. E Cary, Harvard UP, 1925: 7.3A
C Greig, Pliny: *A Selection of his Letters*, CUP, 1978: 5.1B, 6.2B
The *Guardian*, 16th January, 1997: 6.5B
Josephus, *The Jewish War*, ed. E M Smallwood, Penguin, 1981: 3.1C
Livy, *The Early History of Rome*, trans. A De Selincourt, Penguin, 1969: 2.2A
R D MacNaughten (trans.), *Rome, its People, Life and Customs*, McKay, 1963: 6.1C
Martial, *The Twelve Books of Epigrams*, trans. J A Pott and F A Wright, Dutton, 1924: 6.4E
J Nichol, *The Vikings*, Blackwell, 1985: p62
R Nichols and K McLeith, *Through Roman Eyes*, OUP, 1976: 6.2D, 6.6B
QED - The Body in the Bog, BBC Television, 1985: 1.2D, 1.2E
The Sunday Times magazine, 6th April, 1997: 1.2C
Gaius Suetonius Tranquillus, *The Twelve Caesars*, trans. R Graves, The Folio Society, 1957: 1.1C
Tacitus, *The Imperial Annals of Rome*, trans. M Grant, Penguin, 1973: 3.1A, 7.2A, 7.3F, 7.3E,
The Times, 26th September, 1996: 3.3C
J Wilkes, *The Roman Army*, CUP, 1972: 3.3A

Medieval Realms (pages 66–153)

W Anderson (ed. trans.), *Chronicles*, Centaur Press, 1963: 11.1B

Camden Society XXXVII, *A Relation of the Island of England, in about the year 1500*, 1847: 6.5B

John Chancellor, *Edward I*, Weidenfeld and Nicholson, 1981: 7.3A

Geoffrey Chaucer, *The Canterbury Tales*, Penguin, 1962: 3.3A

Ian Ferguson, *History of the Scots*, Oliver and Boyd, 1987: 7.4A

G N Garmonsway (trans.), *The Anglo-Saxon Chronicle*, Dent, 1972: 4.1

W O Hassal, *They saw it Happen 55 BC – 1485*, Blackwell, 1965: 4.3B, 11.4B

Robert Higham and Philip Barker, *Timber Castles*, B T Batsford, 1992: 2.5D

Rosemary Horrocks, *The Black Death*, Manchester University Press, 1994: 9.1C, 9.2A, 9.4A, 9.4B, 9.4E, 9.4F

E M C van Houts, 'The Norman Conquest through European Eyes', *English Historical Review*, 110, 1995: 2.5B

John Joliffe (trans.) *Froissart's Chronicles*, Harville Press, London, 1967: 1.1C, 10.3B

E D Kirk (ed. trans.), *Piers Plowman*, WW Norton, 1990: 10.1A

Tony McAleavy, *Conflict in Ireland*, Holmes McDougal, 1987: 7.2A

Sir Hugh Middleton, *Historical Pamphlets No.4*, Order of St John of Jerusalem, Library Committee, 1930: 3.4C

C Platt, *The English Medieval Town*, Paladin, 1976: 8.2A, 8.2C, 10.1C

Eileen Power, *Medieval Women*, Methuen, 1975: 3.6C

E Revell (ed.) *Later Letters of Peter of Blois*, OUP, 1993: 4.2B

H T Riley (ed.) *Thomae Walsingham Historia Anglicana* in part one of *Chronica Monasterii Sancti Albani*, Rolls Series, 1863-4: 10.3D

Schools Council Project, *Medicine through Time*, Book 3: 8.1B, 11.2C

E Woelfflin (ed. trans.), *Regula Monachorum*, Lipsiae, 1895: 3.4B

The publishers have made every effort to trace copyright holders of material in this book. Any omissions will be rectified in subsequent printings if notice is given to the publisher.

Reed Educational and Professional Publishing Ltd Halley Court, Jordan Hill, Oxford OX2 8EJ

MELBOURNE AUCKLAND FLORENCE PRAGUE MADRID ATHENS SINGAPORE TOKYO SAO PAULO CHICAGO PORTSMOUTH NH MEXICO IBADAN GABORONE JOHANNESBURG KAMPALA NAIROBI

© Fiona Reynoldson and David Taylor 1997

The moral rights of the proprietors have been asserted.

First published 1997

00 99 98 97
10 9 8 7 6 5 4 3 2 1

British Library Cataloguing in Publication Data is available from the British Library on request.

ISBN 0435 30949 8

Designed and produced by Dennis Fairey and Associates Ltd

Illustrated by Richard Berridge, Finbarr O' Connor, John James, Angus McBride, Arthur Phillips, Piers Sanford and Stephen Wisdom.

Printed by Mateu Cromo in Spain

Cover design by Wooden Ark

Cover photographs: *Ministrant Carrying a Tray of Food with Silenus Playing a Lyre and a Young Satyr Playing a Syrinx*, North Wall, Oecuss, 60–50 BC, Courtesy of Villa dei Misteri, Pompeii/Bridgeman Art Library, London. *Massacre of Rebellious French Peasants at Meaux 1358*, Courtesy of e.t. archive.